THE
LAST
KING OF
WALES

T0386659

THE
LAST
KING OF
WALES

GRUFFUDD AP
LLYWELYN C. 1013–1063

MICHAEL & SEAN DAVIES

To our parents, Monica and Jim Davies

First published 2012

The History Press
The Mill, Brimscombe Port
Stroud, Gloucestershire, GL5 2QG
www.thehistorypress.co.uk

British Library Cataloguing in Publication Data.
A catalogue record for this book is available from the British Library.

ISBN 978 0 7524 6460 2

Typesetting and origination by The History Press
Printed in Great Britain

CONTENTS

ABBREVIATIONS

AC	*Annales Cambriae*, ed. J.W. ab Ithel (London, 1860)
Age	Davies, R.R., *The Age of Conquest: Wales, 1063–1415* (Oxford, 1991)
ANS	*Anglo-Norman Studies*
Arch. Camb.	*Archaeologia Cambrensis*
ASC	*Anglo-Saxon Chronicle*, ed. and trans. D. Whitelock (London, 1961). All given dates follow this edition
BBCS	*Bulletin of the Board of Celtic Studies*
Beginnings	Williams, I., *The Beginnings of Welsh Poetry*, ed. R. Bromwich, 2nd edn (Cardiff, 1980)
Bren.	*Brenhinedd y Saeson or The Kings of the Saxons*, ed. and trans. T. Jones (Cardiff, 1971). All year references are to the amended dates given by Jones
Brut (Pen. 20)	*Brut y Tywysogyon or The Chronicle of the Princes, Peniarth MS. 20 Version* , ed. and trans. T. Jones (Cardiff, 1952). All year references are to the amended dates given by Jones
Brut (RBH)	*Brut y Tywysogyon or The Chronicle of the Princes, Red Book of Hergest Version*, ed. and trans. T. Jones (Cardiff, 1955). All year references are to the amended dates given by Jones
CaO	*Culhwch ac Olwen*, ed. R. Bromwich and D. Simon Evans (Cardiff, 1992)
CMCS	*Cambrian/Cambridge Medieval Celtic Studies*

Description	Gerald of Wales, *The Description of Wales,* ed. and trans. L. Thorpe (Harmondsworth, 1978)
EHR	*English Historical Review*
Gruffudd ap Cynan	*A Mediaeval Prince of Wales: The Life of Gruffudd ap Cynan,* ed. and trans. D. Simon Evans (Llanerch, 1990)
HW	J.E. Lloyd, *A History of Wales from the Earliest Times to the Edwardian Conquest,* 2 vols, 3rd edn (London, 1939)
Journey	Gerald of Wales, *The Journey Through Wales,* ed. and trans. L. Thorpe (Harmondsworth, 1978)
JW	*The Chronicle of John of Worcester,* ed. R.R. Darlington, trans. J. Bray and P. McGurk, 3 vols (Oxford, 1995). All given dates follow this edition
Law	*The Law of Hywel Dda,* ed. and trans. D. Jenkins (Llandysul, 1986)
Life of King Edward	*The Life of King Edward (who rests at Westminster, attributed to a monk of Saint Bertin)* ed. and trans. F. Barlow, 2nd edn (Oxford, 1992)
LL	*The Liber Landavensis,* ed. and trans. W.J. Rees (Llandovery, 1840)
Mabinogi	*The Mabinogion,* ed. and trans. J. Gantz (Harmondsworth, 1976)
Map	Walter Map, *De Nugis Curialium/Courtiers' Trifles,* ed. and trans. M.R. James, C.N.L. Brooke and R.A.B. Mynors (Oxford, 1983)
NLWJ	*National Library of Wales Journal*
OV	Orderic Vitalis, *Historia Ecclesiastica,* ed. and trans. M. Chibnall, 6 vols. (Oxford, 1969–80)
TCHS	*Transactions of the Caernarfonshire Historical Society*
THSC	*Transactions of the Honourable Society of Cymmrodorion*
TRHS	*Transactions of the Royal Historical Society*
Triads	*Trioedd Ynys Prydein/The Welsh Triads,* ed. and trans. R. Bromwich, 2nd edn (Cardiff, 1978)
TWNFC	*Transactions of the Woolhope Naturalists Field Club*

Vitae	*Vitae Sanctorum Britanniae et Genealogiae*, ed. and trans. A. W. Wade-Evans (Cardiff, 1944)
WHR	*Welsh History Review*

INTRODUCTION

G RUFFUDD AP LLYWELYN came closer than any other man to becoming the figure for the Welsh that Alfred is to the English, that Charlemagne is to the French and that Kenneth MacAlpin is to the Scots, yet today – on the 1,000-year anniversary of his birth – the would-be nation builder is largely forgotten.[1] Gruffudd united all the territories that comprise modern Wales, conquered land across the border that had been in English hands for centuries, forged alliances with key Anglo-Saxon dynasties and turned the Viking threat to his realm into a powerful weapon in his hands. In 1055, Gruffudd led a great army and fleet against the English border, crushing its defenders, burning Hereford and forcing Edward the Confessor to recognise his status as an under-king within the British Isles, leaving Wales as a united and independent state for the only time in its long history. Having emerged as a war leader, Gruffudd would also prove to be more: a patron of the arts and the Church. He had the trappings of a king, including impressive wealth, courts at Rhuddlan and throughout the country, professional ministers, a powerful household and a strong naval presence. At the height of his powers he was described by a native source in imperial terms as '*rege Grifido monarchia britonum prepollente*' ('King Gruffudd, sole and pre-eminent ruler of the British').[2] Gruffudd's downfall was engineered by Harold Godwinesson, while his eventual betrayal and murder at the hands of his own men – the forebears of the princes who would dominate Wales until the Edwardian Conquest – narrowed the country's political ambitions and left Wales in chaos on the eve of the arrival of the Normans. But the connections between Gruffudd, Harold and

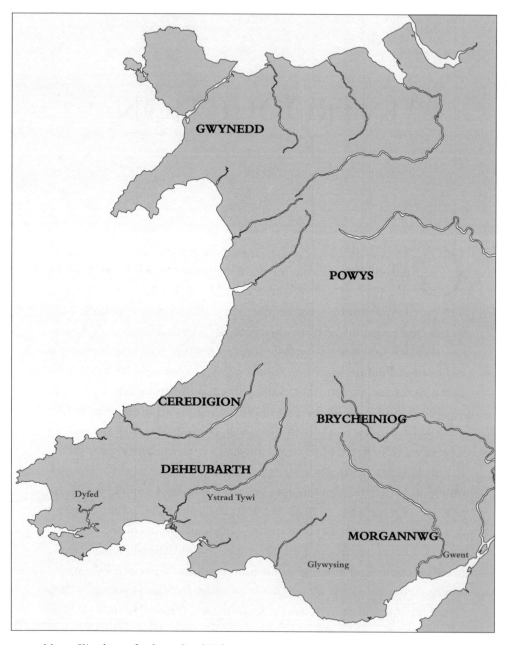

Map 1 Kingdoms of early medieval Wales.

Map 2 Districts of early medieval Wales.

the events of 1066 go far deeper than that. This victory over his great Welsh rival set Harold, the man who would become the last Anglo-Saxon king, on an arrow-like path to his own downfall at Hastings three years later.

Wales in the Early Middle Ages

Gruffudd's reign was at the end of the most neglected period of Welsh history, the 600 years between the departure of the Roman legions from Britain and the arrival of the Normans in 1066. The area that would evolve into modern-day Wales had become territorially defined during the Roman era, with the flexible groupings of kin lands that had developed in prehistoric times coalescing under the empire's administration and then emerging as kingdoms after the legions' withdrawal from the island.[3] The leaders of those petty kingdoms vied with the early Anglo-Saxon war-lords for land and power, but the realistic ambitions of 'Welsh' rulers for pan-British domination were brought to an end in the seventh century.[4] With horizons narrowed, four major kingdoms emerged as the dominant entities within Wales: Powys, Gwynedd, Dyfed/Deheubarth and Glamorgan. Below these over-kingdoms there remained a large number of smaller enti-ties such as Ceredigion, Ystrad Tywi, Brycheiniog, Upper Gwent and Lower Gwent, whose rulers clung to royal nomenclature with varying degrees of success. Such changes mirrored political developments across the rest of post-Roman western Europe, with Wales fitting into a model that could be called proto-feudal. In broadly comparable societies throughout the fallen empire, dominant figures like Charlemagne and Alfred would emerge from the Darwinian maelstrom, establishing the legend and legacy that would lead to the emergence of the great kingdoms of medieval Christendom.

While we must be wary of hindsight in imagining an inevitable move towards such unity in Wales, the country did see a succession of ambitious and able leaders rise to positions of hegemony over much of the modern-day bounds of the country. The obstacles were many, most notably in the south-east, where Glamorgan (a convenient title, but one that does not reflect splits between Glamorgan itself and Upper and Lower Gwent) was resolutely independent. Elsewhere, royal lines were able to project their power over kingdoms outside their original patrimony, but nature, law and custom all played a part in limiting ambitions. Rees Davies described 'a geographically fragmented country ... [where] it was the locality or district which was often the most meaningful and basic unit of loyalty and obligation.'[5] Even today, the central mountain massif is a huge dividing line between north and south Wales, while the medieval traveller would also have to face the problems of poor roads, marshy uplands, fast-flowing rivers and other natural hazards. The difficulties of travel and communication were well known to the twelfth-century writer Gerald of Wales who noted that 'because of its high mountains, deep valleys and extensive forests, not to mention its rivers and marshes, it is not easy of access.'[6] Would-be Welsh dynasts were further hamstrung by the native law of partible inheritance and the acceptance of the idea of many kings as the norm. While there are notable examples of brothers working in harmony, the multitude of potential heirs to patrimonies tended to lead to political carnage, the feuding opening the way for the leading nobles (known as *uchelwyr*) to foster their own independence and influence at the expense of royal power. These problems were not insurmountable, but Welsh kings also had to deal with outside interference from Anglo-Saxon England and sea raiders from Ireland, Scandinavia and the isles, near-neighbours who had easy access to the country and who could bring overwhelming power to bear on Welsh affairs. In the face of all these problems, Wendy Davies noted that: 'There were always people with power in early Wales, but no-one ever had enough.'[7]

Despite the many challenges, it is clear that a Welsh identity did develop in the early Middle Ages, marking the people out as a distinct group in both their own eyes and those of the outside world. Using the language spoken throughout the country, the people called themselves the *Cymry* ('people of the same region'), although the conquering Anglo-Saxons used the term Welsh ('foreigners'). The country's art, law and religion were distinct, unifying factors; institutions that were recognised and fiercely defended from alien interference. Legend and mythology also had a major role to play. The Welsh chronicle would call the most successful rulers of early medieval Wales 'Kings of the Britons', highlighting the persistent idea of a wider realm above the swath of competing kingdoms, waiting for a *Mab Darogan* ('Son of Destiny') to claim it. Idealised pictures of a post-Roman Britain free of the hated Anglo-Saxon invaders were dominant features of verse and literature, a rich vein of material that would be mined by Geoffrey of Monmouth in the twelfth century.

Despite the repeated references to 'Britain', it was clear to all that the realistic political ambitions of a unifying ruler of the Welsh in the early Middle Ages were confined to 'Wales'. The fact was materially outlined with the construction of Offa's Dyke in the eighth century, with the great border earthwork hardening the delineation between Wales and England. The main players on the political stage of Wales in the last two centuries of the first millennium would come from a vibrant new dynasty that exploded onto the scene in the ninth century, displacing royal lines that had dominated since the time of Rome. The new dynasty's founder was Merfyn Frych ap Gwriad, who succeeded to the kingship of Gwynedd in 825. Nothing certain is known about his background, although plausible arguments have been made to suggest that he could have come from a noble line in Powys, from the Isle of Man, or from Manaw Gododdin in the region of modern-day Edinburgh. The fact that Merfyn held Gwynedd until his death in battle

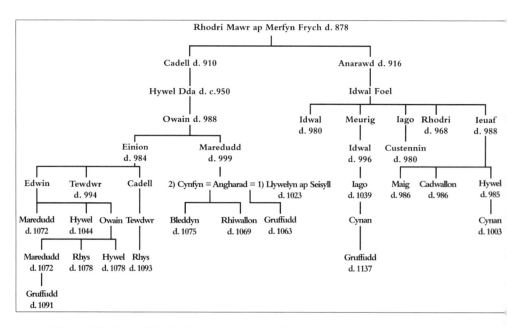

Figure 1 The line of Merfyn Frych in the tenth and eleventh centuries.

in 844 would suggest that he was a capable ruler, and he was succeeded by his son Rhodri Mawr ap Merfyn Frych, whose epithet means 'the Great'. Both Merfyn and Rhodri married into the ancient dynastic line of Powys, helping Gwynedd's claims to hegemony over that ancient kingdom whose old dynastic line came to an end when its last king, Cyngen, died in exile in Rome in 856. Rhodri also projected his power into Ceredigion, attaching the formerly independent kingdom to his realm and opening the way for future expansion into Dyfed.

Rhodri's son and successor, Anarawd, was another king of power and ability who ranged widely across Wales, working in close concert with his brothers. Expansion within Wales was an ongoing ambition of his, despite having to face powerful Anglo-Saxon and Viking threats. Dyfed fell to the sons of Rhodri at the beginning of the tenth century, and Anarawd established his brother Cadell in south Wales while he continued to rule directly in the north. This geographical division of the Merfyn Frych dynasty would be maintained after the deaths of both Anarawd and Cadell, although the latter's son would move out of his Dyfed powerbase to again unite north and south. Hywel ap Cadell – better known as Hywel Dda ('the Good') – became established as a model of ideal kingship for later generations. Although it is difficult to distinguish the contemporary truth of his reign from later legend, Hywel is associated with the revision and codification of Welsh law and is the first known Welsh king to mint his own coins; his handling of relationships with the burgeoning power of Wessex also suggests a statesman of ability. Hywel's death in 949/50 heralded the start of a chaotic period in Welsh politics, a time characterised by rivalry between the southern and northern branches of the Merfyn Frych line along with growing outside interference from Anglo-Saxon and Viking forces. Hywel Dda's grandson, Maredudd ab Owain, was the most prominent leader to emerge, using his powerbase in the south-west to attempt to win dominance over the rest of the country, including the south-east.[8] But his rivals were many, and when he died without an established heir in 999 Wales would enter the new millennium as a land of chaos – and of opportunity.

Llywelyn ap Seisyll

The descendants of Merfyn Frych had dominated Wales since their fore-bear's death in 844 and would play a central role in the country's politics in years to come, but for much of the first century of the new millennium the line would be eclipsed. Maredudd ab Owain lost control of Gwynedd in the last years of his reign, and after his death north and south were again separated. Partible inheritance meant that Gwynedd and Deheubarth – the name given to the consolidated south-western kingdoms of Dyfed and Ystrad Tywi from the start of the tenth century – were themselves divided between members of the ruling dynasties. The descendants of Maredudd's brother Einion ruled in Deheubarth, while members of the northern branch of the Merfyn Frych line held power in Gwynedd. On a local level, it is impossible to determine whether relations within Deheubarth and Gwynedd were harmonious, but internal conflict between the ruling fami-lies seems the most likely scenario. The Welsh chronicle records that Cynan ap Hywel – one of the co-rulers in Gwynedd and a great-great-grandson of Anarawd ap Rhodri Mawr – was 'slain' in 1003, with civil war the most likely explanation.

The native sources are all but silent from 1004 to 1018, but when the Welsh chronicle kicks back into life it is dominated by a new name: Llywelyn ap Seisyll, the father of Gruffudd ap Llywelyn. For the year 1018 it is recorded that Llywelyn killed the otherwise unknown Aeddan ap Blegywryd and his four sons.[9] It seems likely that Llywelyn was already King of Gwynedd in 1018, although neither the date nor manner of his accession can be deter-mined. It could be suggested that he profited from the splits in the Merfyn Frych line and that he played some part in the events surrounding the death of Cynan ap Hywel in 1003, but this can be no more than speculation. Genealogies record that Llywelyn was related to the Merfyn Frych line through his mother, named as Prawst ferch Elise ab Anarawd ap Rhodri Mawr, but this claim is thought to be a late fabrication. Kari Maund traces it to twelfth-century propaganda from the restored Merfyn Frych line that attempted to suggest that legitimate kingship in Wales rested with the descendants of Anarawd ap Rhodri Mawr when, in reality, 'kings in elev-enth century Wales whose ancestry lay outside the Line of Merfyn in the

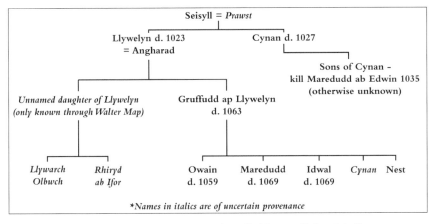

Figure 2 Known and suggested descendants of Gruffudd's grandfather, Seisyll.

male line were not considered in any way anomalous or intrusive by their contemporaries'.[10] It seems likely that Llywelyn was a man who rose by virtue of his own ability, climbing from the ranks of the petty nobility. His origins are unclear but most probably lay in Powys, the ancient kingdom that had been largely subsumed by Gwynedd since the ninth century.[11]

What is certain is that by 1022 Llywelyn was a secure and respected King of Gwynedd and a man pushing wider claims to hegemony within Wales. In its entry for that year the chronicle uses the grandiloquent term 'supreme king of Gwynedd and foremost and most praiseworthy king of all the Britons' to describe Llywelyn. The title 'King of the Britons' had emerged in the Welsh chronicle as a moniker that was reserved for the greatest rulers with the widest ambitions: Anarawd ap Rhodri, Hywel Dda and Maredudd ab Owain. Llywelyn's ambitions in the south are suggested by his marriage (at an unknown date) to Angharad, the daughter of Maredudd ab Owain, and the chronicle entry for 1022 concerns a battle for the control of Deheubarth waged at Abergwili, just outside Carmarthen:

> And then a certain Irishman falsely pretended that he was son to king Maredudd [ab Owain] and he desired to have himself called king. And the men of the south received him as lord over their kingdom; and his name was Rhain. And Llywelyn ap Seisyll, supreme king of Gwynedd and foremost and most praiseworthy king of all the Britons, warred against him. In his time the

old men of the kingdom were wont to say that his territory from the one sea to the other was replete with an abundance of wealth and men, so that it could not be imagined that there was a man either poor or needy in all his lands nor an empty township nor a place of want.

And then Rhain the Irishman vigorously led a host; and, after the manner of the Irish, with presumptuous pride he incited his men to fight; and he confidently promised them that he would prevail. And he came up boldly against his enemies. The latter, however, steadily and fearlessly awaited the swollen, treacherous inciter. He, too, sought the battle boldly and fearlessly; and after the battle had been waged, and a general slaughter had been made on either side, and the men of Gwynedd had fought steadily and bravely, then Rhain the Irishman and his host were defeated; and as is said in the proverb – 'Urge on thy dog, but do not pursue' – he attacked bravely without fear but retreated shamefully after the manner of a fox. And the men of Gwynedd in rage pursued him, slaughtering his host and ravaging the land and plundering every place and harrying it as far as the March. And he never appeared from that time forth. And that battle was at Abergwili. And after that, Eilaf came to the island of Britain. And Dyfed was ravaged and Menevia [St David's] was destroyed.[12]

We cannot be certain who was in control of Deheubarth at the start of 1022, but perhaps the most likely sequence of events would see Llywelyn already ensconced in the south, having projected his power from his northern base. This may have been resented by the local nobility, who turned to Rhain to lead their rebellion. Attempts to identify 'the Irishman' have proved problematical, and, while he may have been a foreign adventurer, David Thornton has suggested that he may have been – as he claimed – a son of Maredudd ab Owain, or at least a Welsh nobleman with well-founded claims to the leadership of Deheubarth.[13] Llywelyn's victory over the so-called 'traitor' reveals more than just military might. The surviving versions of the Welsh chronicle are based on a work that was being written at St David's in the early eleventh century. The chronicle was subject to many influences before it emerged in the extended Welsh-language form quoted above, but its support for the overlordship of the northern king indicates that he was controlling propaganda in the south. The revival of the chronicle in 1018 after its hiatus from 1004 could suggest direct patronage from Llywelyn. Other Welsh rulers, including Gruffudd ap Llywelyn, would give grants of land and other wealth to the Church after victory in war, often in recompense for damage suffered during the conflict.[14] Llywelyn's forces indulged in the punishment ravaging of Deheubarth after the victory over Rhain, but it is likely that Llywelyn then offered generous grants to the Church, the support of the chronicle for his rule suggesting that he had won over the educated class.[15] The subsequent attack on Dyfed and destruction of St David's by Eilaf is difficult to interpret. The Dane, who held an earldom in England under Cnut, may have acted independently. It is also possible that he was intervening in Wales in support of an ally, but if this is the case we cannot determine whether he was on the side of Rhain or Llywelyn. Eilaf is also mentioned in the *Life of St Cadog*, where he is said to have led an attack on the holy man's church at Llancarfan in Glamorgan. This was presumably on his way to, or on his return from, the attack on Dyfed. Glamorgan at the time was under the rule of Rhydderch ab Iestyn, and it is suggested later that Rhydderch was in an alliance with Llywelyn. A new Bishop of Llandaff had been appointed in 1022: a man named Joseph whose clerical family would play a major role in building the authority of the see and who are intimately associated with Llancarfan. If we can ascribe political motives to Eilaf's campaign in Wales, this could suggest that his move was a reaction to Llywelyn's victory at Abergwili and in support of the remaining opposition to Llywelyn and Rhydderch in Deheubarth and Glamorgan.

Llywelyn reached the apogee of his power after Abergwili, but by 1023, just one year later, he was dead, an event significant enough to be recorded, not just by his loyal native scribe, but by the major chroniclers of Ireland. It is likely that Llywelyn was a relatively young man at the time of his death. Our surviving sources betray no hint of foul play in the great king's demise, but the Tudor historian David Powel attributes the death of Llywelyn – and, later, of his brother Cynan (d. 1027) – to the brothers Hywel and Maredudd ab Edwin, direct male descendants of the southern Merfyn Frych line from their great-great-grandfather, Hywel Dda.[16] The Welsh chronicle says that Llywelyn was succeeded in the south by Rhydderch ab Iestyn, a king who had risen to dominance over Glamorgan and was then able to extend his rule to Deheubarth, the first time that a ruler from the south-east had been able to make such a move west.[17] The Book of Llandaff repeatedly claims that Rhydderch was ruling all of Wales at this time, although this problematic source has its own reasons for wanting to emphasise the king's power.[18] Hywel and Maredudd would themselves succeed Rhydderch in Deheubarth when he was killed at the hands of the Irish in 1033.[19] Powel claims that the sons of Edwin hired these Irish mercenaries, although his value as a source is suspect.[20]

An intelligible picture of the period can be discerned, with Llywelyn's position in the south challenged by disgruntled members of the local nobility who had claims to kingship. Rhain may have been such a noble, or he may have come from Ireland, but in his challenge for the throne he made use of military resources from across the Irish Sea.[21] This was a policy continued by the southern noblemen Hywel and Maredudd as they fought for a share of the patrimony. If foul play was involved in the downfall of Llywelyn then these two brothers are prime suspects, and they would also be the natural enemies of Rhydderch ab Iestyn. Llywelyn and Rhydderch were most likely allies in a struggle to control Deheubarth and to make its native kings their clients. The chronicle's praise for Llywelyn, and the fact that Rhydderch succeeded him as king in the south, indicates that the northern king was the senior partner in this alliance. Both Llywelyn and Rhydderch would leave famous sons named Gruffudd who would become kings in Wales. But, rather than co-operation between the two Gruffudds, it would be their conflicts that would do much to shape the future of the country.

Notes

1. The BBC's lavish 2012 television production *The Story of Wales* – intended to trace the 'history of the nation from the Ice Age to the Information Age' – did not even mention Gruffudd, jumping straight from the reign of Hywel Dda (d. 949/50) to 1066.

2. *Liber Landavensis. The Text of the Book of Llan Dav*, ed. J.G. Evans and J. Rhys (Oxford, 1893), p.266; *LL*, pp.535–36.

3. See R. Karl, 'From head of kin to king of a country. The evolution of early feudal society in Wales', in R. Karl, and J. Leskovar (eds), *Interpretierte*

*Eisenzeiten 2. Fallstudien, Methoden, Theorie. Tagungsbeiträge der 2. Linzer
Gespräche zur interpretativen Eisenzeitarchäologie. Studien zur Kulturgeschichte von
Oberösterreich* (Oberösterreichisches Landesmuseum, 2007), pp.153–84; K.R.
Dark, *Civitas to Kingdom: British Political Continuity, 300–800* (Leicester, 1994).

4. In the twelfth century, Geoffrey of Monmouth would claim that the
   title 'King of the Britons' was given up after the death of Cadwaladr the
   Blessed in 682, the original inhabitants of the land then taking on the
   name 'Welsh'.

5. *Age*, p.12.

6. *Description*, p.220.

7. Davies, W., *Patterns of Power in Early Wales* (Oxford, 1990), p.91.

8. See D.E. Thornton, 'Maredudd ab Owain: Most famous king of the Welsh',
   WHR, 18 (1997), 567–91.

9. See *Brut* (Pen. 20), *Brut* (RBH) and *Bren.*, s.a. 1018.

10. See K. Maund, *The Welsh Kings: The Medieval Rulers of Wales* (Stroud, 2004),
    pp.59–63.

11. *Ibid.*; see also *HW*, II, p.359; D. Walker, *Medieval Wales* (Cambridge, 1990), p.17.

12. *Brut* (RBH), s.a. 1022.

13. See D.E. Thornton, 'Who was Rhain the Irishman?', *Studia Celtica*, 34 (2000),
    131–48.

14. See S. Davies, *Welsh Military Institutions, 633–1283* (Cardiff, 2004), pp.250–8.

15. For more on this, see pp.92–4.

16. D. Powel, *The Historie of Cambria* (London, 1584, facsimile edn, Amsterdam,
    1969), pp.86–8. It is possible that Powel had access to additional contempo-
    rary sources that are now lost.

17. Rhydderch's heritage is obscure, but he may have had a family link to
    the rulers of Deheubarth and could have been an uncle of Hywel and
    Maredudd's father, Edwin; see K. Maund, *Ireland, Wales and England in the
    Eleventh Century* (Woodbridge, 1991), pp.20–2.

18. *LL*, pp.518–23. Rhydderch is mentioned in the context of his witnessing of
    grants to the Church. The greater the power that could be attributed to the
    king, the more weight the authority of the charter would be likely to carry.

19. For a discussion of whether these raiders were Irish or Hiberno-
    Scandinavians, see S., Duffy, 'Ostmen, Irish and Welsh in the eleventh
    century', *Peritia*, 9 (1995), 378–96.

20. Powel, *Historie*, p.88. It should also be noted that the fate of Rhain 'the Irishman' is unknown after his defeat at the Battle of Abergwili in 1022 where he may, or may not, have been killed.
21. If Rhain was Maredudd ab Owain's son then he was continuing a strategy that had been used by his father, who is the first known Welsh ruler to employ Viking forces as mercenaries; see Thornton, 'Maredudd', 586.

1

THE EARLY YEARS

T HE EARLIEST YEARS of Gruffudd ap Llywelyn's life are shrouded in obscurity, but an educated guess would date his birth to *c.* 1013. Gruffudd was still a minor when his father met his untimely demise in 1023, indicating that he was not born earlier than *c.* 1007. Gruffudd is Llywelyn's only known son, but Gruffudd had a sister and two younger half-brothers, Bleddyn and Rhiwallon. The brothers were the product of Gruffudd's widowed mother Angharad's later marriage to Cynfyn ap Gwerystan, a nobleman from Powys. Bleddyn and Rhiwallon emerged as the two most prominent leaders of Wales after Gruffudd's demise in 1063, suggesting that they were senior nobility who had held high office during their half-brother's years of glory. Both had their lives prematurely cut short in conflict: Rhiwallon in 1069 and Bleddyn in 1075. Although we cannot be certain of their age at the time of their deaths, this would indicate that both were born *c.* 1024–43 and it would suggest that Angharad's prime childbearing years were in the period *c.* 1010–35. As a terminal date for Gruffudd's birth, his first notice in the native chronicle is in 1039 when he claimed the kingship of Gwynedd. At this time he already held a position of some power and authority within Wales, suggesting that he was probably in his 20s and born no later than *c.* 1019.

Hints about Gruffudd's early years are supplied by the twelfth-century writer Walter Map, who was a product of the Anglo-Norman March of Wales. Map was probably a Welshman who lived and worked in Herefordshire, serving King Henry II and Bishop Gilbert Foliot, and he was a man who eventually rose to the position of Archdeacon of Oxford. His work contains collections of folk tales and anecdotes about the Welsh, some of which are based on native sources. Map's stories about Gruffudd would have been brought to Herefordshire from the neighbouring region of Brycheiniog, an area where the Welsh king was particularly active.[1] The fact that such tales were still current in Map's day, having passed through three generations, is indicative of the impact of Gruffudd's reign. It should be noted though, that Map was not trying to write straight history: his humorous writings are full of exaggerations and need to be treated with caution. He describes Gruffudd as a slothful child who underwent a remarkable youthful transformation after being goaded by his sister:

[Gruffudd] when young, in the reign of his father [Llywelyn], was lazy and sluggish, and sat among the ashes of his father's hearth, a good for nothing and feeble creature, who never went out. Often had his sister reproached him, and on the eve of the Circumcision [1 January] she came to him with tears and said: 'Dear brother, it is to the great shame of the king and of this realm that you are become a scorn and a byword to everyone, you who are the only son and heir of the king. And now I beseech you to go out and do something which is very easy and quite without risk. It is a custom in this country that tonight, which is the first night of the year, all the young should go out to raid and steal, or at least to listen, that each may make trial of himself thereby: to raid, like Gestinus who went far afield quietly and without trouble brought back what he seized, and all that year flourished with a series of successes: to steal, like Golenus the bard who brought a straw from a pigsty without raising a single grunt, and that year was able to steal whatever he liked without complaint or noise; and to listen or eavesdrop like Theudus [Theodosius] who stole privily to the house of Meilerius and heard one of those who sat within say: "This morning I saw a little cloud rising out of the sea and it became a great cloud so that it covered the whole sea," and going thence he considered that he – a little one – was the little cloud, risen out of the sea and was to become king: and this the event proved. Now then, dear brother, do you go out at least to listen, which you can do without any risk.' The boy, awakened by this, as if his soul were roused from a heavy sleep, and rising to a mood before unknown to him, became instinct with strength, agile, quick and ready of resolve, and calling to him a number of companions, placed himself by the wall of someone's house in secret, with attentive ears. Many were sitting within, and waiting for the cooking of a bullock cut up in their midst, which their cook was stirring about in a pot on the fire with a flesh-hook, and said the cook: 'I have found one very strange piece among the rest; I am always pushing it down and putting it under the others, and in a moment it turns up above them all.' 'That,' said [Gruffudd], 'is myself, whom many have tried and will try to keep down, but I shall always break out mightily, against all their wills.'[2]

While we can place only limited historical value on the facts of this tale, it is a story worthy of comparison to the legends that built up around Alfred burning the cakes or Robert Bruce observing a persistent spider's attempts to spin a web in a damp cave. The survival of the tale indicates that folklore and mythology were building up around Gruffudd in the century after his death, signs of the impact that his reign had made in Wales and across the border. Such tales thrived even though Gruffudd had not founded a dynasty to nurture and develop propaganda about the deeds of his epic reign.

Blunting the Horns of Wales

Map's writings contain traditions that can be related to the political realities faced by the young Gruffudd. It has been seen that, after Llywelyn ap Seisyll's death, Deheubarth was contested between Rhydderch ab Iestyn and the sons of Edwin, Hywel and Maredudd.[3] Gwynedd, meanwhile, passed to Iago ab Idwal, a member of the northern branch of the Merfyn Frych dynasty, although the chronicle does not date the start of his reign until 1033. This was the year that Rhydderch ab Iestyn was killed, and the Book of Llandaff claims that the latter had been 'ruling over all Wales' with the exception of the island of 'Euonia' (probably Anglesey) that was in the hands of Iago.[4] Llywelyn's family had not disappeared from the scene, and may have been ruling at least a part of the northern kingdom. Llywelyn's brother, Cynan, was the senior representative of the dynasty whose powerbase, it has been suggested, was in Powys.[5] The chronicle records that Cynan was 'slain' in 1027, and this has been associated with an attempt he may have made to win power in Gwynedd.[6] Another explanation is equally possible though: the Tudor historian David Powel claims that the sons of Edwin were responsible for Cynan's downfall. If this is true, his death can be seen as part of the ongoing battle for control of Deheubarth. Rhydderch ab Iestyn's slaying in 1033 was followed a year later by conflict between his sons and the sons of Edwin at the Battle of Hiraethwy, the location and result of which is unknown. In 1035, Maredudd ab Edwin was killed by the otherwise unknown sons of Cynan. They are thought to be the offspring of Cynan ap Seisyll, and their action could be seen as revenge for the killing of their father by Maredudd and Hywel.

The name of Gruffudd ap Llywelyn is notably absent from this record of political violence in the late 1020s and early 1030s, most likely a testament to his youth and, possibly, to Map's picture of a 'lazy and sluggish' child. Map's description of the bobbing meat is followed by this passage:

> Gladdened by so plain an omen he left his father, proclaimed war on his neighbours, and became a most crafty and formidable raider of others' goods; every band of scoundrels flocked pell-mell to him, and in no long time he was feared even by his father, after whose death he peaceably possessed all the bounds of Wales – peaceably, that is, but for the tyrannies he inflicted on his subjects. For he resembled Alexander of Macedon and all others in whom covetous lust destroys self-control, liberal, vigilant, quick, bold, courteous, affable, extravagant, pertinacious, untrustworthy, and cruel.[7]

Map's description of the political scene cannot be taken literally. The idea of Gruffudd being militarily active during his father's lifetime does not accord with the chronology of other sources, and we must remember that it was not the writer's intention to deliver an accurate historical record.[8] The passage would make more sense if the 'father' referred to was actually a foster father. It was accepted Welsh royal practice to send noble sons to the court of a fellow king or magnate for their education, a custom that reflected great honour on the foster father. Gerald of Wales, a twelfth-century product of the Anglo-Norman conquest of Pembrokeshire, believed that the institution contributed to incessant Welsh political and dynastic feuding:

[A] serious cause of dissension is the habit of the Welsh princes of entrusting the education of each of their sons to a different nobleman living in their territory. If the prince happens to die, each nobleman plots and plans to enforce the succession of his own foster-child and to make sure that he is preferred to the other brothers. The most frightful disturbances occur in their territories as a result, people being murdered, brothers killing each other and even putting each other's eyes out, for as everyone knows from experience it is very difficult to settle disputes of this sort.[9]

It is possible that Gruffudd was raised in such a fashion after the death of Llywelyn, with Cynfyn ap Gwerystan, Cynan ap Seisyll and even Rhydderch ab Iestyn potential candidates to have been entrusted with the foster-father role.

Map's account of Gruffudd's activities in his early adolescence accords with what we know of the lives of other young and ambitious Welsh nobles. Gruffudd's raiding of his neighbours is described with a chiding air by the clerical writer, but if a leader were to prove his military skill he needed to display ability in this field. Ravaging, evasion and ambush were the key components of medieval warfare, a fact obscured by the overemphasis that has been placed on the role of the so-called 'decisive battle'.[10] The winning and distributing of spoil was the main way for a leader to build and maintain the support of his most important institution: his military household or *teulu*.[11] The Welsh laws describe the *teulu* as one of the three 'indispensables' of a king.[12] In the prose tale *Culhwch and Olwen* – a work that is thought to have been first written down in the eleventh century and that was undoubtedly told in the courts of the day – King Arthur makes a speech declaring: 'We are noble men so long as others come to us, and the more gifts we distribute, the greater will be our reputation and fame and glory.'[13] The *Life of St Cadog* was also first written down in the eleventh century, although it purports to describe sixth-century events. In one passage the nobles of St Cadog's father Gwynllyw, a notable military leader, complained when his religious son abstained from 'feasting, playing dice and other activities of the household … What means this religion of our son? We were expecting the increase of our kingdom from him, who by his preaching destroys our household. Let us force him to warfare, because he knows better than us how to rule the people.'[14] The Welsh chronicle describes a typical raiding foray in 1110, when the outlawed Owain ap Cadwgan was running wild with his followers in Ceredigion:

> And his [Owain's] comrades went on forays to Dyfed and they plundered the land and seized the people and carried them off with them ... On another occasion they summoned 'hotheads' [W. ynfydion] from Ceredigion to add to the numbers along with them, and by night they came to a township of Dyfed and slew all that they found, and despoiled others and carried others off with them as prisoners to the ships, and thence sold them to their folk. And after burning the houses and killing the animals and carrying others off with them, they returned to Ceredigion.[15]

Map's description of 'scoundrels flocking pell-mell' to join Gruffudd ap Llywelyn in his early years could be echoed by the Welsh chronicle's use of the term 'hotheads' or 'imbeciles'. Ynfydion was a term applied to the followers of both Owain in 1110 and those of Gruffudd ap Rhys in 1116, and it has been suggested that this was because they had disregarded the traditional bonds of society.[16] Both Owain ap Cadwgan and Gruffudd ap Rhys broke 'horizontal' ties of lordship within Wales by attracting men from regions not under their own lordship. Rees Davies saw these 'hotheads' as the equivalent of the class of juvenes on the continent who drove feudal violence: young, restless men who were of the military class but without a patrimony, and who were, therefore, seeking glory, a livelihood and, above all, the chance to win land by joining the household of a lord of promise and ability.[17] A youthful Gruffudd ap Llywelyn would have sought to recruit the best military talent to his household in order to fulfil his boundless ambition. The chroniclers were able to denigrate the 'hotheads' of 1110 and 1116 because of the ultimate failure of their ambitions. The men who chose to follow Gruffudd ap Llywelyn did not suffer such disappointment and hence avoided the censure of later writers.

The early years in the political careers of successful medieval Welsh kings were often dripping in blood, but there are suggestions that even by those standards Gruffudd's formative period was brutal. Walter Map continues thus:

Whatever young man he saw of good and strong promise, by some craft he either murdered him or maimed him to prevent his attaining manly strength, ever mindful of his own safety; and very quickly he became supreme, and this was his saying: 'I kill no-one, but I blunt the horns of Wales, that they may not hurt their mother.' Now Llywarch, nephew of [Gruffudd], a boy of good abilities, tall and handsome, who attained great successes and showed many signs of strength and worth, was one who, the king foreboded, would become great, and he feared for himself, and, vainly, tempted him with assiduous flattery. After long seeking he found him in a spot where the boy had no cause to fear for his safety, and said: 'Tell me, my dear one, why you should fly me, who am the surest of refuges for you and yours? It is an obstacle that you put in your own way and that of all your family, and there is nothing that can atone for the shame you put on yourself, but that kindly intercourse should join you to me who am already one with you in blood: if you have any fear of me, I will give you any sureties you may choose.' 'Then,' said the boy, 'I name as surety Hoel, whom you caused to be smothered in secret when he was upon your errand; Rotheric, whom you left-handedly received with a kiss and embrace and slew with a knife, Theodosius, whom as he walked and talked with you you tripped up with your foot and cast down the sheer rocks; and your nephew Meilin, whom you privily seized by guile and let him die loaded with chains in a dungeon'; and in like manner he reminded him of many more whom he had destroyed.[18]

Again we should not look for absolute historical accuracy in the names or events of this story, although there is another intriguing reference to a man named Llywarch in Gruffudd's immediate entourage.[19] It seems unlikely that Gruffudd's supposed mutilation and destruction of close family members in his rise to power refers to the offspring of his only known brothers, Bleddyn and Rhiwallon. They were younger than the king and are thought to have been supporters of Gruffudd's in his years of glory. The tale may preserve a kernel of truth regarding the manner of Gruffudd's rise to power and his treatment of other family, however. Map uniquely claims that Gruffudd had a sister, but we know no more of her and there is no certain record of any descendants.[20] It is notable that there is no mention of Gruffudd's first cousins, the sons of Cynan ap Seisyll, after their killing of Maredudd ab Edwin in 1035. Gruffudd may have seen such capable and established military men as rivals for control of the family's client nobles and lands, and he may have chosen to 'blunt their horns' in order to facilitate his own rise.[21]

Gruffudd Seizes Power

Gruffudd had been busy sharpening his own horns and – whatever the nature of his climb to prominence – by the late 1030s he was an accepted and established figure on the Welsh political scene. This was made clear in 1039 when he first attracted the attention of the native chronicle:

> Iago, king of Gwynedd was slain. And in his place ruled Gruffudd ap Llywelyn ap Seisyll; and he, from his beginning to the end, pursued the Saxons and the other Gentiles and slaughtered and destroyed them, and defeated them in a great number of battles. He fought his first battle at Rhyd-y-groes on the Severn, and there he prevailed. In that year he pillaged Llanbadarn and held rule over Deheubarth and he expelled Hywel ab Edwin from his territory.[22]

Gruffudd is not specifically implicated in the slaying of Iago ab Idwal in the most reliable versions of the Welsh chronicle, but the fact that he was the chief beneficiary means that supposition is inevitable.[23] The key to the question of guilt in the elimination of Iago may lie in the equally puzzling problem faced in trying to identify Gruffudd's own killer in 1063. The strong suggestion is that Iago's son Cynan – who was driven out of Wales to Ireland after his father's death – was heavily involved in this.[24] But, even if we leave this debate aside for the moment, strong circumstantial evidence associated with the events of 1039 intimates that Gruffudd played a part in the destruction of the reigning King of Gwynedd. In his formative years Gruffudd had ruthlessly constructed a local powerbase and recruited the best available military talent, and an aggressive takeover of Gwynedd would seem to be the logical next step. Moreover, the speed of Gruffudd's actions after Iago's death suggests a well-prepared and expertly executed plan designed to regain his father's position as the supreme king in Wales.

His actions are not those of a lucky chancer who simply seized on Iago's timely demise.

Gruffudd immediately felt confident in his newly won power in the north, and his security there would not waver until the final year of his reign. This was not enough for the assertive new ruler, however. Soon after Gruffudd was named as king there was action against the Anglo-Saxons on the eastern borders of Powys: the Battle of Rhyd-y-groes. The name is contained in all versions of the Welsh chronicle and translates as 'ford of the cross' on the Severn. The focus of the Anglo-Saxon military elite would have been on the succession dispute between Harold Harefoot and Harthacnut, but the decision to engage Gruffudd may have been prompted by the death of Elystan Glodrydd, a Powysian magnate with English affinities whose descendants would later enjoy prominence in Builth.[25] The tradition that Elystan was buried at Trelystan, on the slope of the Long Mountain (W. *Cefn Digoll*) to the east of Welshpool, is of note because this is in the region where the Battle of Rhyd-y-groes was fought. Lewys Dwnn, a Welsh poet and genealogist of the Tudor period, claimed that Elystan was slain in a 'civil brawl' at Cefn Digoll. It can be suggested that Gruffudd had removed a rival to his dominance in Powys, but that his Anglo-Saxon neighbours had lost a friendly ally and been left with a powerful and dangerous new enemy on their border. The forces arrayed against Gruffudd indicate how gravely his challenge was regarded, the army being led by the brother of one of the most powerful noblemen in England and two royal thegns. But the *Anglo-Saxon Chronicle* records that the attempt to check Gruffudd was in vain: 'The Welsh killed Edwin, Earl Leofric [of Mercia]'s brother, and Thorkil and Ælfgeat and very many good men with them.'[26] Additional information on the 1039 battle can be gleaned from the writings of a man who was, like Walter Map, a cleric of the Anglo-Norman period with close connections to the Welsh border. John of Worcester compiled his work in the first half of the twelfth century, making plentiful use of the *Anglo-Saxon Chronicle* but also being able to call on other sources and local traditions. In dealing with the later events of 1052, John follows his description of another victory by Gruffudd over the Anglo-Saxons with the line: 'This battle took place on the same day as that when, 13 years earlier, the Welsh killed Edwin, brother of Earl Leofric, in an ambush.' The memory of Rhyd-y-groes had seared itself onto the defeated side's consciousness as its exact date was remembered thirteen years later. This is also noted by the *Anglo-Saxon Chronicle*, but John provides the additional information that Gruffudd's victory was facilitated by an 'ambush'. This was an acceptable and admired tactic in the warfare of the day, and it again suggests the military skill of Gruffudd and the professionalism of the force that he had built around him.[27] With the Welsh king expecting an English response after Elystan's death, a river ford on a traditional invasion route into Wales would have been an ideal place to plot such a stratagem.

Numerous attempts have been made to locate the battle site of Rhyd-y-groes more definitively. Upton-on-Severn in Worcestershire is the most easterly suggestion, but this would place the battle too far across the border.[28] A more plausible argument can be made for the ancient ford across the Severn at Buttington, a few miles to the east of Welshpool. This fits with John Edward Lloyd's suggestion that Rhyd-y-groes was 'near Gungrog and Cefn Digoll', where Elystan was buried.[29] In 1838, 400 skulls that displayed evidence of violent death were discovered in three pits in All Saints churchyard, located within an ancient rectilinear earthwork fortification and just a few hundred metres from the ford. These remains are usually associated with a battle fought at Buttington in 893 when an Anglo-Welsh army besieged and then defeated a Danish host, but a connection with Gruffudd's victory in 1039 cannot be ruled out.

Montgomeryshire antiquaries contended that Rhyd-y-groes was a little further south, in the parish of Forden between Montgomery and Welshpool. Perhaps the most likely location is 3 miles east of Forden, on the modern-day border between England and Wales, a little below Montgomery and the hill where the castle of Hen Domen was constructed in the early 1070s. The name Rhyd-y-groes has been preserved in a farm that is now a caravan site, just to the east of Offa's Dyke, a location that would define Gruffudd's border policy of asserting his authority into 'English' territory. A bridge on the A490 over the River Camlad straddles the border on the site of a ford. The waterway, a tributary of the nearby Severn, has been connected with the final battle said to have been fought by King Arthur: the Battle of Camlann. A further connection to Arthurian legend is that this seems to be the Rhyd-y-groes mentioned in the twelfth- or thirteenth-century Welsh medieval prose tale *The Dream of Rhonabwy*. In that story the location is a meeting point for King Arthur's forces in the build-up to the epic fifth- or sixth-century Battle of Badon. The framework for the tale is twelfth-century Powys, but it is reasonable to assume that the author regarded the site of a famous Welsh victory over the Anglo-Saxons in the previous century as a suitable setting for his narrative. The work bemoans the weak and feeble men of the day who are left to defend the land of the 'Britons', comparing them unfavourably with the great warriors of the past.

The year 1039 had already been an *annus mirabilis* for Gruffudd, but still the Welsh king was not satisfied. With his crushing victory at Rhyd-y-groes having secured his eastern flank against English interference, the son of Llywelyn immediately turned to the task of re-establishing the authority that his father had enjoyed over Deheubarth. It was a bloody challenge that would enflame south-west Wales for the next five years.

Notes

1. See J.E. Lloyd, 'Wales and the coming of the Normans', *THSC* (1899–1900), 122–79.

2. Map, pp. 189–91.

3. See pp. 19–20.

4. *LL*, pp. 518–19. As has been noted, the Book of Llandaff is a problematic source with its own editorial agenda that must always be considered.

5. See pp. 16–17.

6. Maund, *Welsh Kings*, p. 61.

7. Map, p. 191.

8. Map's unreliability as a pure historical source is shown as he repeatedly calls Gruffudd by the name of his father, Llywelyn. It is obvious that the son is the subject of the work.

9. *Description*, p. 261. The practice of fostering out sons is well attested in Welsh law and literature of the period.

10. See, for example, J. France, *Western Warfare in the Age of the Crusades, 1000–1300* (London, 1999) pp. 1–15; J. Gillingham, 'William the Bastard at War', in C. Harper-Bill (ed.), *Studies in Medieval History Presented to R. Allen Brown* (Woodbridge, 1989); M. Strickland, *War and Chivalry: The Conduct and Perception of War in England and Normandy, 1066–1217* (Cambridge, 1996); S. Davies, *Welsh Military*, pp. 86–142.

11. For more on the *teulu*, see *ibid.*, pp. 14–49; S. Davies, 'The *Teulu c.* 633–1283', *WHR*, 21 (2003), 413–54.

12. *Law*, p. 39; see also p. 11.

13. *CaO*, pp. 5–6.

14. *Vitae*, p. 35.

15. *Brut* (Pen. 20), s.a. 1110.

16. R.S. Babcock, 'Imbeciles and Normans: The *ynfydion* of Gruffudd ap Rhys reconsidered', *The Haskins Society Journal*, 4 (1992), 1–8. See also S. Davies, *Welsh Military*, pp. 22, 47–8.

17. R.R. Davies, *Domination and Conquest* (Cambridge, 1990).

18. Map, pp. 191–3.

19. For discussion see pp. 84, 119.

20. The *Life of St Gwynllyw* refers to a nephew of Gruffudd's, 'Rhiryd ab Ifor', who is depicted serving as a high-ranking officer of the king in south-east Wales in the early 1060s. It is possible that this man was the son of Gruffudd's sister, or of another, unknown sibling. For further discussion, see pp. 84, 110. Rhirid was the name given to another of Gruffudd's nephews, one of Bleddyn's sons who was killed in 1081. It is also possible that Gruffudd was married to the daughter of a man named Rhirid, see p. 96.

21. Map's story could also be related to Gruffudd's later rise to power and his treatment of rival Welsh kings. In the narrow dynastic world of Welsh politics, they are likely to have been linked by blood to Gruffudd, although they would not have had the intimate family associations suggested by Map.

22. *Brut* (RBH), s.a. 1039. See also *Brut* (Pen. 20), s.a. 1039; *Bren.* s.a. 1039.

23. One of the Welsh-language redactions of the chronicle, known as *Brenhinedd y Saesson*, does name Gruffudd as Iago's killer. But it is difficult to rely on the minutiae of this problematic text when it does not agree with the generally more accepted Welsh-language versions of the lost Latin original – *Peniarth MS. 20* and *Red Book of Hergest* – nor with the related Latin chronicle, the *Annales Cambriae*.

24. For discussion, see pp. 118–20.

25. C.A.R. Radford and W.J. Hemp, 'The cross-slabs at Llanrhaiadr-ym-Mochnant', *Arch. Camb.*, 106 (1957), 109–16; Maund, *Ireland*, pp. 45–8, 106.

26. *ASC* (C), 1039; see also JW, 1039.

27. See S. Davies, *Welsh Military*, pp. 55, 118. William the Conqueror was admired for such a tactic at the Battle of Varaville in 1057. The duke had been shadowing the army of King Henry I of France and Geoffrey Martel and, when his opponents were crossing the River Dives, William was able to cut off and defeat its rear section to win a famous victory; see also J. Gillingham, 'William the Bastard at War', in C. Harper-Bill, C.J. Holdsworth and J.L. Nelson (eds), *Studies in Medieval History Presented to R. Allen Brown* (Boydell, 1989), p. 153.

28. For the story of how this location came to be suggested, see J.E. Lloyd, 'Wales and the coming ', 129.

29. Radford and Hemp, 'The cross-slabs', 114–15; *HW*, II, p. 360, fn 4; also his 'Wales and the coming', 129–30.

2

THE BATTLE FOR
DEHEUBARTH

FTER GRUFFUDD'S TRIUMPH on the battlefield at Rhyd-y-groes
he immediately marched west, following the River Severn towards
its source in Plynlimon. The Welsh chronicle then recounts his pil-
laging of the monastery of Llanbadarn Fawr near Aberystwyth, a wealthy
religious community that had attracted the attention of Viking raiders in
988.[1] Its resources were undoubtedly a boost to Gruffudd's expansive plans
and would have been welcomed by his army, but the attack had a much
deeper significance. Welsh kings would attack religious institutions that
were throwing their weight behind dynastic rivals, as in 978 when Hywel
ab Ieuaf ravaged Clynnog Fawr because the community was supporting his
enemy and uncle, Iago ab Idwal.[2] Hywel's display of power was a sign of the
way that the conflict was flowing, and in the following year he was able to
capture Iago and take possession of his land.[3] In contemporary Ireland, the
plundering and burning of a rival's monasteries was a standard part of an
attack on his power.[4] Llanbadarn Fawr may have been a significant military
presence in its own right; in the twelfth century, Gerald of Wales was out-
raged at the secular nature of the monastery, where the abbot performed his
church duties with a spear in his hand, surrounded by about twenty armed
warriors.[5] Gruffudd's strike against Llanbadarn in 1039 was his first direct
move against Hywel ab Edwin as he sought to wrest control of Deheubarth
from the southern king. The more serious blow had already been landed
at Rhyd-y-groes as Hywel – like Elystan Glodrydd – had affinities with
Anglo-Saxon nobility, and possibly even a landed power base across the
border. The speed of Gruffudd's victory, followed by his descent on Hywel's

territory, had caught the southern king completely off balance and, in the words of the Welsh chronicle, Gruffudd 'held rule over Deheubarth and he expelled Hywel ab Edwin from his territory'.[6]

The political situation was not quite as straightforward as was suggested by the chronicle, however, and Hywel remained very much an active player in south Wales. It seems that, while Gruffudd had taken control of Ceredigion and Ystrad Tywi, Hywel retained his hold on Dyfed in the far south-west, a refuge that gave him access to the military resources of Ireland. The chronicle entry for 1041 records: 'The battle of Pencadair [Pencader] took place; and there Gruffudd defeated Hywel, and he seized his wife and took her for his own.'[7] Pencader is 10 miles north of Carmarthen, close to the spot where Dyfed, Ceredigion and Ystrad Tywi meet, and its strategic value is shown by the fact that it was chosen by the Anglo-Norman lord Gilbert de Clare as the site for a castle in 1145.[8] Gruffudd's appropriation of his rival's wife after the battle adds a juicy personal touch to the bitter feud, and could suggest that Hywel had been caught by surprise at one of his royal courts. Gruffudd may have been following a policy engaged in by his father and grandfather in marrying into the southern nobility. His actions could also be related to a story told by Map of the northern king's jealousy of his 'very beautiful wife' whom he 'loved more ardently than she loved him', although this could equally refer to another of Gruffudd's partners.[9]

Hywel had suffered a humiliating defeat, but he maintained his authority in the south-west. In 1042 the chronicle records him winning a famous victory at Pwlldyfach, 5 miles north-west of Carmarthen, over a Viking horde that had been ravaging Dyfed. Gruffudd had trouble of his own from sea raiders in 1042, as, immediately after the description of Hywel's victory at Pwlldyfach, the chronicle records that the northern king was captured 'by the Gentiles of Dublin'. It could be suggested that these were in some way allied to Hywel, or that the move was engineered by Cynan ab Iago, the son of the man who Gruffudd had replaced as king of Gwynedd. The latter claim was made by the sixteenth-century Welsh historian David Powel and the seventeenth-century Irish historian James Ware. Powel claimed to have had access to versions of the Welsh chronicle that are now lost, but much of his unique information looks suspiciously like he was filling in gaps in the chronicle with supposition, meaning that the antiquarian sources need

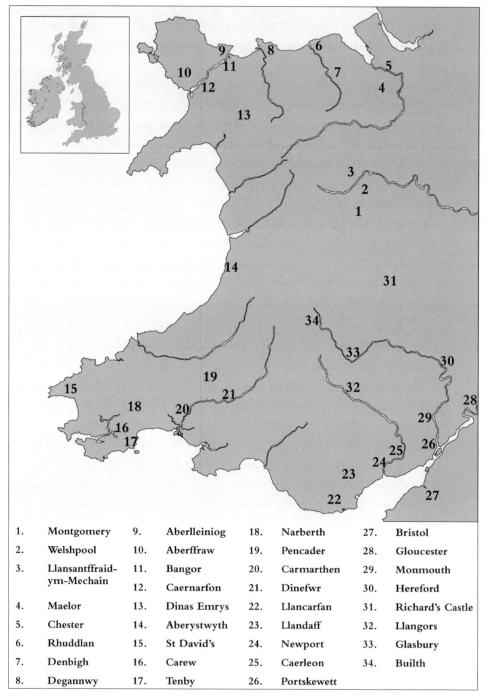

Map 3 Key locations in Wales and the borders mentioned in the text.

1.	Montgomery	9.	Aberlleiniog	18.	Narberth	27.	Bristol
2.	Welshpool	10.	Aberffraw	19.	Pencader	28.	Gloucester
3.	Llansantffraid-ym-Mechain	11.	Bangor	20.	Carmarthen	29.	Monmouth
		12.	Caernarfon	21.	Dinefwr	30.	Hereford
4.	Maelor	13.	Dinas Emrys	22.	Llancarfan	31.	Richard's Castle
5.	Chester	14.	Aberystwyth	23.	Llandaff	32.	Llangors
6.	Rhuddlan	15.	St David's	24.	Newport	33.	Glasbury
7.	Denbigh	16.	Carew	25.	Caerleon	34.	Builth
8.	Degannwy	17.	Tenby	26.	Portskewett		

to be handled with great care. Powel and Ware each claim that Cynan and his Irish mercenaries treacherously captured Gruffudd, but that when they tried to return to their ships they were attacked by an army of Gruffudd's supporters who freed their king and forced the enemy back across the sea. The Welsh chronicle's reference to the raiders coming from Dublin is certainly intriguing, given the fact that the descendants of Iago are known to have lived in exile there.[10] Whatever the truth of the matter, Gruffudd's capture had few long-term consequences. Our next notice of his activity comes in 1044 when he was holding sole dominion over Deheubarth, with his great rival Hywel in exile in Ireland. The struggle between the two men was reaching a crescendo, with Hywel again calling on his allies from Ireland to try to regain his lost dominion in Wales. The chronicle says that he gathered a fleet of the 'Gentiles of Ireland' to ravage Deheubarth, making his entry into the country by sailing up the Tywi towards Carmarthen:

> And Gruffudd ap Llywelyn encountered him; and there was a mighty battle and many of the host of the foreigners and of his own host were slain at the mouth of the River Tywi. And there Hywel was slain and Gruffudd prevailed.[11]

The Two Gruffudds

The victory at the mouth of the Tywi was the crowning achievement of a remarkable five years for Gruffudd since he first entered the historical record in 1039. He was now ruling over Powys, Gwynedd and Deheubarth and was in an arguably unprecedented position of power for a Welsh king. It is also likely that he enjoyed friendly relations with the obdurately independent region of south-east Wales, given that his family and that of Rhydderch ab Iestyn had faced a common enemy in the form of Hywel ab Edwin. But such a commanding position brought its own problems for Gruffudd. Local nobility throughout Wales remained proudly independent and conscious of their own prerogatives and claims to dominion. Throughout the medieval world, the only way to rule was to win the personal support of such local magnates and their military followings. In Wales these leading men, many of whom had forefathers who would have been called kings in an earlier age, were known as *uchelwyr*.[12] Such men could choose alternative would-be kings from within their ranks to challenge an overlord who was unpopular, over-mighty, incapable, or who had not delivered what they felt was an appropriate reward for their loyalty. They could also look to Ireland and to England for potential allies, and leaders in both of these neighbouring lands had good reason for wanting to see Wales remain a divided, feuding territory. Gruffudd's newly won hegemony would be rocked by two challenges from within Wales that were described by the native chronicle as 'deceit' and 'treachery', and the *uchelwyr* were at the heart of each event.

The first of these challenges came in 1045, and it arose from an unlikely source. The dynasties of Llywelyn ap Seisyll and Rhydderch ab Iestyn had found common cause against their mutual enemies, the sons of Edwin. But, the year after Gruffudd killed Hywel ab Edwin, the chronicle records the first known instance of discord between the two families: 'There was great deceit and treachery between Gruffudd and Rhys, the sons of Rhydderch, and Gruffudd ap Llywelyn.'[13] Perhaps the best explanation for the conflict is that the sons of Rhydderch had been in alliance with Gruffudd ap Llywelyn, but after the death of Hywel they did not receive the rewards that they had anticipated from the senior party in the alliance. On the strength of this chronicle entry and evidence from John of Worcester, historians have drawn some broad conclusions concerning the balance of power in south Wales at that time. In 1049 and 1053, John describes Gruffudd ap Rhydderch as 'King of the Southern Britons' (L. *regis Australium Brytonum*) and in a posthumous reference in 1065 as 'King of the South Welsh' (L. *regis Suth-uuallanorum*). It has, therefore, been assumed that the death of Hywel ab Edwin opened the way for the line of Rhydderch ab Iestyn to return to power in Deheubarth and that – for the next ten years – it was Gruffudd ap Rhydderch rather than Gruffudd ap Llywelyn who held dominion in the south.[14] This, though, is hard to reconcile with the position of power that was held in Deheubarth by Gruffudd ap Llywelyn in 1044; a status that he had won by ruthless campaigning over a five-year period. It seems inconceivable that the chronicle's brief and vague notice of 'great deceit and treachery' in 1045 would be enough to cause Gruffudd to abandon the south for the best part of a decade.

At this time the Welsh chronicle was being written in St David's, but it took little interest in Gruffudd ap Rhydderch. Apart from the 1045 entry, the only other direct reference to him is on his death (although he is also likely to have been one of the 'sons of Rhydderch' said to have fought the sons of Edwin in 1034). The chronicle never claims that he ruled over Deheubarth, unlike his father Rhydderch ab Iestyn who is specifically said to have done so, and never claims that anyone took Deheubarth from Gruffudd ap Llywelyn after he won it in 1039. John of Worcester's mentions of Gruffudd ap Rhydderch also need to be handled with care, as his references to 'South Wales' seem to refer to the south-east, excluding Deheubarth. Walter Map was capable of making this distinction between *Sudwallia* and *Deheubard*, one example being his description of Gelligaer (Glamorgan) as being in *Sudwallia*.[15] Welsh writers of Latin had other terms to describe Deheubarth, the *Annales Cambriae* calling Rhydderch ab Iestyn 'King of the right-handed [Western] Britons' (L. *regnum dextralium Brytonum*).[16] The closest comparison to John of Worcester's description of Gruffudd ap Rhydderch as 'King of the Southern Britons' (L. *regis Australium Brytonum*) can be found in the *Life of St Gwynllyw*, a work first written down in south-east Wales in the late eleventh century. Its author sees Gwynllŵg – a *cantref* to the east of the River Rhymney that incorporates modern-day Newport – as the seat of the king of *Australium Brytonum*.[17] Perhaps the definitive evidence comes from John of Worcester himself: he mentions Gruffudd ap Llywelyn on more occasions than Gruffudd ap Rhydderch and calls the former by the more exalted term of 'King of the Welsh' (L. *Rex Walanorum*), suggesting that the 'King of the Southern Welsh' title was primarily designed to distinguish Gruffudd ap Rhydderch from his northern namesake.[18] John does not even consider the death of Gruffudd ap Rhydderch worth recording in 1055, instead referring to it incidentally in his entry for 1065.

The fact that Gruffudd ap Rhydderch was noticed at all in English sources marks him as a ruler of some power and importance, but the records that we have signal his main areas of activity as being in the south-east, and it is likely that his origins lay in Ergyng and Upper Gwent (*Gwent Uwch-coed*).[19] In the period 1045–55 he was battling to secure a wider hegemony over the south-east, not ranging widely across Deheubarth in opposition to Gruffudd ap Llywelyn. It is possible that his raid on southern Gwent in

1049 in alliance with a fleet of Hiberno-Scandinavians was a strike against Meurig ap Hywel of Glamorgan, who had annexed Lower Gwent (*Gwent Is-coed*).[20] From Gwent, Gruffudd ap Rhydderch and his allies crossed the Wye, attacked the manor of Tidenham and defeated an English force under Bishop Aldred.[21] Kari Maund suggests that the charter describing Gruffudd ap Rhydderch as 'King of Glamorgan' (L. *Rex Morcanhuc*) was linked to this victory over the English, perhaps as a thanksgiving.[22] With these events securing his overlordship of Glamorgan, Gruffudd ap Rhydderch was active on the Gloucestershire border in the 1050s.[23] His brother, Rhys, was slain at the instigation of King Edward in January 1053, apparently in revenge for the border raids. Gwent would certainly become the main area of activity for Gruffudd ap Rhydderch's son, Caradog. In 1065 he destroyed Harold Godwinesson's hunting lodge at Portskewett near Caerwent, he was probably the Caradog responsible for the destruction of villages in Domesday Book survey of Gloucestershire, and he was described as being 'from Gwent Uwch-coed' and enjoying the support of the 'men of Glamorgan'.[24]

Treachery in Ystrad Tywi

Gruffudd ap Llywelyn was ruling in Deheubarth throughout this period, but it is possible that the growing power of Gruffudd ap Rhydderch provided an external focal point for leading men of the region who were dissatisfied with their king. The fact that there were dissatisfied subjects in Deheubarth was shown by the events of 1047 when 'about seven score men of Gruffudd ap Llywelyn's warband were slain through the treachery of the leading men of Ystrad Tywi'.[25] This bald statement needs to be put into context to understand the calamity that had struck the king. The central importance of a warband to its ruler has been stressed; its members were his closest family, his most trusted friends and his best military talent. The warband always stayed close to its lord, and if 140 of its members had been slaughtered then Gruffudd himself was surely close to being caught in the trap. The number of casualties was staggering. Estimating the size of the household of a Welsh lord is extremely problematical, but it has been suggested that around fifty men could be the average.[26] Gruffudd had lost nearly three times that number, yet his power was not broken. This suggests that his household force alone still numbered in the hundreds after the disaster.

Gruffudd's casualties do seem to have prompted a change in policy, one that shows his vision and flexibility as a leader. He would later form alliances with the key power brokers in Glamorgan,[27] and it is possible that the relationships were instigated at this time. More tellingly, up until this point the Welsh king had relied upon the native military resources that he had fostered from his youth; whenever he had encountered forces from England and Ireland, Gruffudd was on the opposing side. Now though, the *Anglo-Saxon Chronicle* describes Earl Swegn of Herefordshire taking hostages from Wales after a ravaging raid made in alliance with Gruffudd ap Llywelyn.[28] The Welsh chronicle makes no mention of Anglo-Saxon involvement, but says that after the slaughter of his men Gruffudd ravaged the lands of Ystrad Tywi and Dyfed in order to avenge his losses. Swegn was the eldest son of Earl Godwine of Wessex, the most powerful nobleman in Edward the Confessor's England. The son was a major landowner in his own right, Swegn's territory including holdings that bordered on Gruffudd ap Rhydderch's sphere of dominion in south-east Wales. It has been suggested that Gruffudd ap Llywelyn and his new ally used the opportunity to attack the southern Gruffudd, but there is nothing to support this in the sources and Gruffudd ap Rhydderch's first recorded raid across the English border was not until 1049. Gruffudd ap Llywelyn would later make more significant use of Anglo-Saxon alliances and may have helped Swegn in 1051–52, but the 1047 experiment was cut short because of the instability of the latter's character. On his way home after his Welsh foray, Swegn seduced and abducted the Abbess of Leominster. He chose to abandon his earldom, apparently because he could not marry the abbess, and was exiled by Edward. The disgraced nobleman spent time in exile in Denmark and Flanders and harried the English coast with a fleet. Swegn had a chance to regain a legitimate place amongst the English nobility in 1049, but his treacherous slaying of his cousin Earl Beorn left him as a man of 'no honour' – an outcast.[29]

Gruffudd ap Llywelyn's cultivation of Anglo-Saxon alliances would have to wait as, within Wales, his targeting of Ystrad Tywi and Dyfed for revenge ravaging showed that opposition to his rule was still focused in the old strongholds of Hywel ab Edwin in the south-west. Those regions suffered gravely for their actions, as Gruffudd's campaign was followed by a particularly harsh winter in 1047/48 when 'there was very great snows on the Calends of January and it remained until the feast of Patrick'.[30] The woes of the south were not over as, in 1049, the Welsh chronicle says that 'all of Deheubarth' was laid waste by ravaging. This event should be related to the activity of a fleet of thirty-six Hiberno-Scandinavian ships mentioned by John of Worcester and the *Anglo-Saxon Chronicle*. Peter Sawyer has estimated that a Viking ship of the period would carry about forty men, giving the raiding force a formidable potential size of around 1,500 men.[31] One of the surviving texts of *Annales Cambriae* uniquely records that the ravaging was done by the people of Deheubarth themselves as part of a scorched earth policy because of fear of the 'Gentiles'.[32] This would fit with a picture of the rebellious lands of Dyfed and Ystrad Tywi seeking to follow the traditions of Hywel ab Edwin and his forefathers in welcoming Viking mercenaries. These forces would have combined to attack areas of Deheubarth that were more secure under the rule of Gruffudd ap Llywelyn. Such a threat was grave even to a king as powerful as Gruffudd, and Deheubarth suffered significantly. But the defence of the province was effective, and by August 1049 the fleet had moved on to south-east Wales in search of easier pickings. The raiders made land at the mouth of the Severn (Portskewett a likely location), and joined forces with Gruffudd ap Rhydderch, who used the opportunity to secure his hold on Glamorgan and to raid the English border.[33]

The repeated Hiberno-Scandinavian interferences in Wales had proved the biggest danger of all to Gruffudd ap Llywelyn's continued rule in Deheubarth. It is possible that the aggrieved Dublin exile Cynan ab Iago had played a role in this, but the raiders themselves had a strong interest in keeping Wales weak and divided, and the profits gained from lucrative slave raiding should be seen as a prime motivation behind the attacks.[34] In 1052, the Welsh chronicle records that a fleet coming from Ireland to Deheubarth foundered, an attack that the antiquarians Powel and Ware again connected with Cynan ab Iago. Kari Maund has made an intriguing alternate link between this force and the flight of the supporters of King Eachmarcach of Dublin following the takeover of the city by Diarmait mac Máel na mBó

of Leinster.[35] In any case, the destruction of the fleet finally gave Gruffudd
the breathing space he needed to fully subdue the lands he had conquered
in the south, and there is no further notice of discord in Deheubarth until
the final months of his reign. The report of the ravaging of the south in 1049
and the foundering of the fleet from Ireland in 1052 are the only entries in
the Welsh chronicle in the period 1048–55, suggesting a period of internal
peace. Gruffudd's restless energy was far from quelled, though, and with his
increased security in the south he turned his attention east, setting his sights
on the ambitious target of expansion across the English border.

Notes

1. For an indication of the potential material gains from the monastery, see H.
   Pryce, 'Ecclesiastical Wealth in Early Medieval Wales', in N. Edwards and A.
   Lane (eds.), *The Early Church in Wales and the West* (Oxford, 1992), pp.22–32.
2. *Brut* (RBH), s.a. 978; K. Maund, 'Dynastic Segmentation and Gwynedd
   c. 950–*c.* 1000', *Studia Celtica*, 32 (1998), 155–67.
3. *Brut* (RBH), s.a. 979.
4. D. Ó'Cróinín, *Early Medieval Ireland, 400–1200* (Harlow, 1995), p.278.
5. *Journey*, p.180. For discussion of the possible military service owed from
   Church lands, see S. Davies, *Welsh Military*, pp.79–81.
6. *Brut* (RBH), s.a. 1039.
7. *Brut* (Pen. 20), s.a. 1041.
8. It was also the site where Rhys ap Gruffudd ('The Lord Rhys') submitted to
   Henry II in 1163. Gerald of Wales suggested the wildness of the countryside
   around Pencader in the twelfth century; *Journey*, p.140. For further discussion of the history of fortification at the site, see R. Turvey, 'The defences of
   twelfth-century Deheubarth and the castle strategy of the Lord Rhys', *Arch.
   Camb.*, 144 (1995), 103–32, 107.
9. *Map*, pp.186–9.
10. This is explored further on pp.44, 108, 118–20.
11. *Brut* (Pen. 20), s.a. 1044.
12. See S. Davies, *Welsh Military*, pp.75–9.
13. *Brut* (Pen. 20), s.a. 1045.
14. See, for example, Lloyd, 'Wales and the coming', 133; D. Walker, 'A note on
    Gruffudd ap Llywelyn', *WHR*, 1 (1960–63), 83–94; W. Davies, *Patterns*, p.37;

idem, *Wales*, p.103; Maund, *Ireland*, p.67; *idem*, 'The Welsh Alliances of Earl Ælfgar and his family in the mid-eleventh century', *ANS*, 11 (1988), 182.

15. Map, p.150, n.2; p.198.

16. *AC*, p.23. It has been argued that 'right-handed Wales' originally meant the whole of south Wales but that it came to exclude Gwent and Glamorgan in the south-east; see L. Thorpe (ed.), *Gerald of Wales: The Journey through Wales and the Description of Wales* (Harmondsworth, 1978), p.94, n.97.

17. *Vitae*, p.173.

18. JW, pp.566, 576, 580, 584, 596. On one occasion Gruffudd ap Llywelyn is described as 'King of the North Welsh' (L. *Griffinus rex North-Walanorum*), but this was simply to avoid confusion when describing his 1055 showdown with Gruffudd ap Rhydderch; see Maund, *Ireland*, p.133.

19. The Book of Llandaff claims that Gruffudd and his father Rhydderch witnessed grants of land in this region; see also *HW*, II, p.361, n.7; Maund, *Ireland*, p.27.

20. *Liber Landavensis. The Text of the Book of Llan Dav*, p. 255b. See also Lloyd, 'Wales and the coming', 146, n.1; B.G. Charles, *Old Norse Relations with Wales* (Cardiff, 1934), p.44.

21. JW, pp.550–3; see also *ASC* (D), p.114.

22. Maund, *Ireland*, p.197; see also *LL*, p.533.

23. *ASC* (C), p.125; JW, p.573; see also *HW*, II, p.363.

24. *ASC* (C & D), p.137; JW, p.555; Domesday Book, 'Gloucestershire', f. 162a; *Gruffudd ap Cynan*, p.66; see also A.G. Williams, 'Norman lordship in south-east Wales during the reign of William I', *WHR*, 16 (1993), 449, 452.

25. *Brut* (Pen. 20), 1047.

26. S. Davies, *Welsh Military*, pp.22–6.

27. See pp.63, 82–3, 93. It is intriguing to note that at some, unknown point in this era the relics and claims to power associated with St Teilo were trans-ferred from their original home at Llandeilo Fawr in the Tywi valley to Llandaff.

28. *ASC* (C), p.109.

29. See F. Stenton, *Anglo-Saxon England* (Oxford, 2001), pp.429–30.

30. *Brut* (RBH), s.a. 1047–48.

31. P.H. Sawyer, *The Age of the Vikings*, 2nd edn (London, 1971).

32. *AC* (C), p.169.

33. For more on Portskewett, see pp. 55, 80n, 87, 111, 129.

34. See P. Holm, 'The slave trade of Dublin, ninth–twelfth centuries', *Peritia*, 5 (1986), 317–45; D. Wyatt, 'Gruffudd ap Cynan and the Hiberno-Norse World', *WHR*, 19 (1999), 595–617. Viking interest in Welsh slave raiding would only increase in the late eleventh century as the growing power of England made that land a more difficult target and the native Irish conquest of Dublin in 1052 limited opportunity at home.

35. Maund, *Ireland*, pp. 164–5.

3

THE YEARS OF GLORY

WITH DEHEUBARTH FINALLY secured after over a decade of conflict, Gruffudd ap Llywelyn turned his attention to the England-Wales border where he would seek plunder, territorial aggrandisement and, perhaps most importantly, security. His first strike was in 1052, the Welsh king having mobilised forces for another season of campaigning in south-west Wales but having his hand freed when the Hiberno-Scandinavian fleet heading from Ireland to Deheubarth foundered. Gruffudd fought a battle on the thirteenth anniversary of Rhyd-y-groes and it is possible that the date of the great, landmark victory had taken on a cultural significance in his reign, prompting the new campaign. Most important, though, was the divided political situation in England, with Gruffudd seizing on the opportunity of a weakened border and, perhaps, acting in support of his old ally, Swegn.

England Divided

The chain of events needs to be traced back to the accession of Edward the Confessor to the English throne in 1042. The new king had been raised in Normandy, the land of his mother, and found himself something of an outsider in an English political landscape that was dominated by three earls: Godwine of Wessex, Leofric of Mercia and Siward of Northumbria. Godwine was the most powerful of the three, a man who had risen to power under Cnut, the Danish king who had supplanted Edward's family on the

English throne. The year after Cnut's death in 1035, Edward had come to England from Normandy. At the same time his brother, Alfred, arrived in a separate expedition. Both brought military support from their homeland in northern France and were part of the opposition to the disputed succession of the new king, Harold Harefoot, but as Alfred moved on London he was betrayed and captured by Godwine. Alfred was blinded and later died of the wounds, while his Norman troops were slaughtered. Edward fled back to Normandy – never to forget Godwine's actions. When he first succeeded to the throne, however, Edward was a little-known king from a foreign land and he had no hope of taking on the most powerful magnate in the realm. The new monarch bided his time, even marrying Godwine's daughter Edith in 1045, and when Godwine secured the return from exile of his disgraced son Swegn in 1051 the family's territorial power base was at its greatest extent. Nevertheless, the Godwines were isolated from the other two most powerful nobles in England, Leofric and Siward, and in the meantime Edward had been steadily building up his own loyal following. The king had turned to people from his homeland, his patronage of the Norman Church and of Norman knights enflaming English opinion. In 1051, with the backing of Leofric and Siward, Edward was at last strong enough to move against Godwine. After a face-off between the military forces of the two sides, the earl and his family were driven into exile. Godwine fled to Flanders with his sons Swegn, Tostig and Gyrth, while another two sons, Harold and Leofwine, headed to Ireland.[1]

Edward used the opportunity to strengthen the Norman presence in England, causing further unrest over alien rule that was exacerbated by poor governance. Duke William of Normandy came to England in the winter of 1051/52, and at this point Edward may have offered him the throne as his successor. The most powerful Norman in England at the time, however, was Edward's nephew, Ralf de Mantes, a man who would come to symbolise all that the native Anglo-Saxons despised about the outsiders who were monopolising the king's patronage. Sometime between 1047 and 1050, Edward made Ralf the new Earl of Herefordshire in place of the exiled Swegn, and Ralf set about reorganising the area's defence, using a model he was familiar with from the continent.[2] The rivalry between Ralf and Swegn in Herefordshire has been suggested as a flashpoint for all the problems that arose in 1051.[3] Anglo-Saxon sources gave Ralf the epithet 'the Timid', but according to Frank Stenton: 'So far as can be seen [Ralf] was the real founder of the system of organised castle building which under the Norman kings made Herefordshire a principal bulwark of the Midlands against assault from Wales.'[4]

On his eastern border Gruffudd had lost his ally, Swegn, and had seen a new earl arrive with ambitious plans to construct fortifications and revitalise the military capability of Herefordshire. The Welsh king may have been alarmed, but he was presented with a window of opportunity for action before Ralf's defensive reorganisation was complete. Edward expected Godwine to invade in early 1052 and ordered a fleet to be manned at Sandwich under the command of Ralf and Earl Odda.[5] Ralf was still on defence duty on the Kent coast at the time of the Welsh attack on Herefordshire, as it was in the immediate aftermath of Gruffudd's raid that Harold returned from Ireland and linked up with Godwine.[6] In the absence of Earl Ralf, Gruffudd drove into northern Herefordshire. Although the attack received no mention in the St David's-based Welsh chronicle it was well recorded by the *Anglo-Saxon Chronicle*: 'Gruffudd the Welsh king was ravaging in Herefordshire so that he came quite close to Leominster, and people gathered against him, both natives and the Frenchmen from the castle. And very good Englishmen were killed and French too. It was the same day that Edwin and his colleagues had been killed 13 years before [in Gruffudd's victory at Rhyd-y-groes].'[7] Gruffudd had marched through Shropshire into Herefordshire, following the line of the Roman road, with the castle named likely to have been Richard's Castle. Domesday Book records that much of south-west Shropshire and north-west Herefordshire were subject to severe wasting prior to 1066, a fact that equates well with Gruffudd's raiding and the likelihood that the lands under the Welsh king's control were butting directly into these border regions.[8]

The attack is likely to have played a part in helping the Godwines back to power in England, but it did not return Swegn to Herefordshire. After his final exile in 1051, Godwine's enigmatic eldest son had embarked on a pilgrimage to Jerusalem and was to die on the return journey, sometime between 1052 and 1053. More border conflict was recorded by the 'C' version of the *Anglo-Saxon Chronicle* in 1053: 'Welshmen killed a great number of Englishmen of the patrols near Westbury.' Westbury in Shropshire is about halfway between Welshpool and Shrewsbury, and if the attack was there it would again highlight the danger that Gruffudd posed in this area of the border. There is also a Westbury-on-Severn in Gloucestershire however, and the clash may have occurred there. If so, the Welsh forces are likely to have been led by Gruffudd ap Rhydderch. He would have the motivation for such a strike as his brother, Rhys, had been assassinated by order of King Edward the previous winter.

A New Alliance

Gruffudd ap Llywelyn had already demonstrated his ability to handle Viking raiders, the vulnerability of England's border defences and the potential gains to be won by exploiting the splits in the Anglo-Saxon political world. In 1055 he would bring all of these elements together to stunning effect. With Swegn dead and a hostile Earl Ralf on his border, Gruffudd ap Llywelyn turned to a most unlikely source as a new ally. The leaders of Mercia were the historic enemies of Wales and in 1039 Earl Leofric had seen his brother, Edwin, killed by Gruffudd at Rhyd-y-groes. But the relentless rise of the Godwine family in England after 1052 saw traditional enmities put aside for the formation of a strong and lasting alliance between Leofric's son, Ælfgar, and Gruffudd.

The rivalry between the houses of Leofric and Godwine had a long history. Under Cnut, Leofric and his father, Leofwine, were the last survivors of the traditional Anglo-Saxon leaders amongst the major aristocracy. Godwine's family was long established as minor nobility in England before the eleventh century, but Godwine himself rose to greatness under service to the Danish king. Frank Stenton contrasted the 'noble, upright and respected' Leofric with Godwine who 'had no ancestral claims to political influence; he could be unscrupulous in action, and the career of aggrandizement he opened to his family accounts in great part for the sense of strain and unrest which colours the reign of Edward the Confessor.'[9] The families repeatedly found themselves at the opposite end of the political divide, as in the dispute over Cnut's successor in 1035–36 and the debate on whether to send military aid to maintain Denmark's independence from Norway in 1047. Leofric supported the exile of the Godwines in 1051, and as a result his son, Ælfgar, was made Earl of East Anglia in place of Godwine's son, Harold.

The return of the Godwines saw Harold restored to East Anglia, but when Godwine died in 1053 and Harold succeeded him as Earl of Wessex, Ælfgar was returned to East Anglia in his place. The events of 1052 had effectively broken the power of Edward's Norman supporters in England and the Godwines gradually assumed control of royal prerogatives. Such a situation would have alarmed Leofric's house, particularly after 1055. In that year the third major earl in England, Siward of Northumbria, died. His eldest son, Osbeorn, had been killed in battle against King Macbeth of Scotland in 1054 and as his next son, Waltheof, was a minor, Siward was succeeded as Earl of Northumbria by Harold's brother, Tostig. It was soon after the elevation of Tostig that the simmering rivalry between the houses of Godwine and Leofric boiled over, with Ælfgar forced into exile in March 1055 for 'treason'. The three extant versions of the *Anglo-Saxon Chronicle* are of little help in trying to determine the facts of the case: the first version is hostile to the Godwines and says that Ælfgar was exiled even though he had not committed any crime; the second is loyal to the Godwines and claims that the earl was guilty of an unnamed act of treason to which he confessed; the third, later, version tries to conflate the two earlier texts and ends up fudging the issue of Ælfgar's guilt. The nature of the supposed crime remains unclear, but it was surely related to Ælfgar's dealings with Gruffudd. In his rivalry with the house of Godwine, Ælfgar, who was destined to succeed his ageing father as Earl of Mercia, sought to build up a western power bloc, putting aside any previous difficulties that his family had experienced with the Welsh king in order to secure a powerful new ally.

Swegn is the only member of the house of Godwine who Gruffudd is known to have enjoyed friendly relations with, and it was not in the Welsh king's interests to see England dominated by a single, over-mighty family.[10] The significance of Gruffudd's search for a strong ally amongst the Anglo-Saxon nobility would become clearer as his ambitions for territorial expansion were revealed. The Welsh king was eyeing the rich lowlands of his eastern border; territories with surviving people amongst their populations who regarded themselves as Britons in terms of language, custom and law. The Welsh had been fighting a rearguard action for control of such land for centuries, with the Anglo-Saxon rulers of Mercia their main enemies. Gruffudd would now reverse this trend and secure Mercia as the bulwark to protect his vulnerable conquests from the direct power of the Anglo-Saxon state. It is likely that the difficult negotiations needed for such a deal between Ælfgar and Gruffudd were brokered by a prominent Welsh nobleman who had a foot in both camps, an individual known by the nickname of Rhys 'Sais' ('the Englishman'). Rhys is the first man known to have been given the title 'Sais', although the moniker – meant to denote someone who could speak English, had been to England, had English parents and/or admired and imitated English ways – would later become fairly common in Welsh sources.[11] Rhys's wife and mother are known to have been Welsh, his family had been prominent in the border regions for generations, and it is possible that he was a distant relation of Gruffudd's. Domesday Book and the genealogies identify him as 'Rhys Sais of Faelor', locating his home at Maelor in the north-west of Shropshire. He held the manor of Erbistock on the western side of a U-bend in the River Dee, near a ford on the England-Wales border that would have been a natural place to hold negotiations. Rhys died in 1070, but his diplomatic service proved a model for his family who performed such duties between Wales and England in the twelfth and thirteenth centuries. The preliminary discussions that Rhys brokered between Gruffudd and Ælfgar bore fruit soon after the earl's exile, John of Worcester recording that the latter:

> went to Ireland, and returned when he had acquired 18 pirate ships and approached Gruffudd, king of the Welsh, to request help against King Edward. Gruffudd at once assembled a large army from his whole realm, and commanded Ælfgar to hurry to meet him and his force with his own troops at the place appointed; having joined forces they entered Herefordshire with the intention of laying waste the English borders.[12]

Wales United

These events were dramatic enough, but the English sources neglect to mention the first act of the campaign that was recorded in the Welsh chronicle: Gruffudd ap Llywelyn's slaying of Gruffudd ap Rhydderch, which resulted in his conquest of south-east Wales. This act and the raid on Herefordshire have traditionally been regarded as separate events.[13] But the power of Gruffudd ap Rhydderch and the self-reliance of south-east Wales have been stressed, and it seems that Gruffudd ap Llywelyn had needed to plan and nurture his strategy of conquest for a number of years. The region had a reputation for obdurate independence that can be traced back to the start of the historical period and the Silures, a warlike tribe who long resisted the Roman advance into the area. After the departure of the legions the little-known native kings of the south-east maintained a rule that was always separate from the other major over-kingdoms of Wales: Gwynedd, Powys and Dyfed/Deheubarth. In 1055 the area was ruled by one of its most powerful and well-documented kings – Gruffudd ap Rhydderch – but in 1055, Gruffudd ap Llywelyn finally had the firepower he needed to overcome his namesake and forge a kingdom of all Wales.

The northern Gruffudd's numerous clashes with Hiberno-Scandinavian fleets had secured Wales a measure of security from sea raiders, with the foundering of the 1052 flotilla heading to Deheubarth being the only notice of their activity in the country in the period 1050–55. Given this, the raiders would look for other opportunities to win plunder and slaves, and the exiled Ælfgar was soon able to muster a mercenary host in Ireland. The reference to eighteen ships would suggest a force of around 750 warriors that – added to Ælfgar's own military household, which accompanied him into exile – would have boosted his army to over 1,000 men. This formidable host played a subordinate role to Gruffudd though, who 'commanded' their actions and had assembled a 'large army from his whole realm'. This reference to a force that has some suggestion of a 'national' levy is extremely rare in Welsh medieval sources. It is likely that other Welsh rulers such as Anarawd ap Rhodri had led armies with some such characteristics, but the previous evidenced example refers to Cadwallon ap Cadfan (d. 633) and the next after Gruffudd would be Llywelyn ab Iorwerth (d. 1240).[14] At the core of the force would have been Gruffudd's own military household (W. *teulu*), well supported by the leading nobles from throughout his lands who owed allegiance to the king and who would have brought their own households with them. In addition to these military professionals, Gruffudd would have gathered a select levy of his realm to fill out his army (W. *llu*). These recruits were fulfilling duties owed to the king by the territorialised military system laid out in the laws of the country, although it seems likely that there would have been room for practical negotiation around the following legal defini-tion: 'The king is not entitled to have from his country any hostings outside its limits save once in each year, and he is not entitled to be in that save for a fortnight and a month. In his own country it is free for him when he likes.'[15] The mechanics of the muster are lost in the mists of time, but it is likely that Gruffudd moved south through Wales, picking up recruits at strategic points known as *maerdrefi* ('royal townships'), where the local organisation would have been handled by the *teulu* of the region's noble. The idealised model in the laws sees the basic unit of land administration as the *tref*, which can be loosely translated as 'township', 'village' or 'settlement'. There were fifty of these in a commote, and each commote had a *maerdref* that tended to be asso-ciated with some sort of (typically light) fortification. Logistics are likely to have played the biggest part in restricting the numbers that Gruffudd would have recruited, but Welsh laws and literature make clear the importance of pack horses, and native leaders were capable of providing supplies for signifi-cant armies.[16] Given that Gruffudd played the lead role in his alliance with Ælfgar, it is likely that the Welsh king's host numbered around 2,500, giving a combined force of around 3,500 men. The significance of such a host can be seen in context when it is considered that estimates of the size of each of the opposing armies at Hastings in 1066 tend to be around 7,000 fighting men.

With such formidable land and sea forces at his disposal, Gruffudd chose to crush and destroy Gruffudd ap Rhydderch. It is likely that he also exploited local rivalries in the south-east, allying with Gruffudd ap Rhydderch's rivals from Glamorgan, including Meurig ap Hywel.[17] The northern king used a pincer movement, travelling overland to the assigned meeting place with Ælfgar and his fleet, which – given the later movements of the force – is likely to have been somewhere near the mouth of the River Wye, possibly Portskewett. For the fleet to be used effectively in the forthcoming assault on Hereford, an attack through Gwent and Archenfield would have been necessary, and this accords with the notice in Domesday Book of the wasting of Archenfield by King Gruffudd.[18] At this time the river was navigable up to and beyond Hereford itself, and the lower Wye ran through territory that would have been under the control of Gruffudd ap Rhydderch. The manner of the death of the southern king is unknown, but he was unable to resist the powerful multi-pronged attack that was sent against him, and the Welsh chronicle records that 'Gruffudd ap Llywelyn slew Gruffudd ap Rhydderch. And after that, Gruffudd ap Llywelyn moved a host against the Saxons, and he arrayed his army at Hereford.'[19]

Hereford Aflame

The subsequent attack on Hereford was in support of Gruffudd ap Llywelyn's ally, Ælfgar, and offered the opportunity for the Welsh to win rich booty. Given the breadth of ambition that the Welsh king had already shown, it is also likely to have had an even more significant goal. Archenfield was a district of southern and western Herefordshire with very strong Welsh attachments, a part of the larger post-Roman kingdom of Ergyng that had been overwhelmed by the Mercians in the course of the eighth century. People regarding themselves as Welsh with their own language, traditions and laws remained in the area, and Gruffudd, as king of all Wales, felt that he had a claim to dominion there.[20] Hereford itself had a particular significance, both in practical and symbolic terms. The Welsh chronicle records a battle between the 'Britons and Saxons' at Henffordd (Hereford) in 760, while sometime around 930 King Athelstan, arguably the most dominant of all the Anglo-Saxon kings in his dealings with Wales, compelled nearly all the Welsh kings of his day to gather to his court in the town. According to the twelfth-century writer William of Malmesbury, Athelstan imposed on them a huge annual tribute of 20lbs of gold, 300lbs of silver, 25,000 oxen plus large numbers of hounds and hawks. Moreover, the meeting resulted in the agreement that the River Wye would form the boundary between Welsh and English people in the region of Hereford. It was probably soon after this that a document was created that was intended to bring about the peaceful settlement of disputes between Welshmen and Englishmen on either side of the Wye in the region, a group of people who were collectively known as Dunsæte.[21] These events have been suggested as a catalyst for the composition of the poem 'Armes Prydein', a work that envisaged a grand alliance against Athelstan by the Welsh, Irish, the Danes of Dublin, the Scots, and the Britons of Strathclyde, Cornwall and Brittany to drive the 'Saxons' out of the country.[22] All of this provided strong cultural and symbolic reasons for Gruffudd to target Hereford, while on a more practical level the town was the capital of the shire and, as such, was crucial to the mustering and deployment of the local defence levy.

As he moved into Herefordshire, Gruffudd would have kept the main body of his army close to his fleet on the River Wye; a devastating attack by land and water that terrified the inhabitants of the country. The defeat of Gruffudd ap Rhydderch had opened up the entry to the river, allowing Gruffudd ap Llywelyn to attack from the south and bypass the new network of castles that protected northern Herefordshire. When William fitz Osbern was made Earl of Hereford in 1067, one of his first acts was to build castles at the river mouth at Chepstow and further upstream at Monmouth, suggesting the need to control access to the Wye and that an awareness of the danger remained fresh in the minds of the locals. The course taken by the fleet is indicated by the fact that at the end of the year's campaign it sailed from near Billingsley, just south of Hereford.[23] The 1055 attack on the town itself is recalled in detail by both English and Welsh sources, marking it as a major event that would live long in the memory of generations to come. The Welsh chronicle glories in Gruffudd's actions after he had arrayed his army against the defending force outside the town:

> Against him rose up the Saxons, and with them a mighty host and with [Earl Ralf] as their leader; and they drew up their army and prepared for battle. And Gruffudd, fearless and with a well-ordered army, fell upon them; and after bitter-fierce fighting the Saxons, unable to withstand the onslaught of the Britons, turned to flight after a great slaughter of them. And Gruffudd pursued them to within the walls of Hereford, and there he massacred them and destroyed the walls and burned the town. And with vast spoil he returned home eminently worthy.[24]

Anglo-Saxon sources describe the scale of the disaster, while tending to focus on the failings of the border defences and Earl Ralf, political splits within the defenders' ranks and the brutality of the victors' treatment of the church at Hereford. John of Worcester presents this vivid account:

> Having joined forces they [Gruffudd and Ælfgar] entered Herefordshire with the intention of laying waste the English borders. Against them the timorous Earl Ralf, son of King Edward's sister, mustered an army and, meeting them on 24 October two miles from the city of Hereford, he ordered the English, contrary to custom, to fight on horseback, but when they were about to join battle, the earl with his French and nobles was the first to take flight. The English, seeing this, followed their commander in flight. Almost the whole of the enemy army pursued them, and slew 400 or 500 of them and wounded many. Then, having gained the victory, King Gruffudd and Earl Ælfgar entered Hereford, slew the seven canons who had held the doors of the main basilica, burnt the minster which Æthelstan, God's Christian bishop, had built with all the ornaments and the relics of Saint Æthelberht, king and martyr, and of other saints, killed many citizens, took many captives, despoiled and burned the city, and returned enriched with a lavish quantity of booty.[25]

These accounts of the battle seem to be at odds with each other; the Welsh sources describing a hard-fought battle while the Anglo-Saxon evidence suggests that Earl Ralf and his army fled almost immediately. This can again be related to the political landscape of England, with native sources there hostile to the foreigners brought in by King Edward, a division that cannot have helped the army's performance at the place of slaughter. The passage has been used to support the idea that Anglo-Saxon forces never fought from horseback, a failing that was also said to have played a part in their defeat by the Normans at Hastings in 1066. This can be questioned, however. We know that the highly professional Anglo-Saxon military forces rode horses to battle and used the animals for supply purposes. In 1062–63 both Harold and Tostig would lead mounted troops into Wales when campaigning against Gruffudd. It is likely that the Anglo-Saxons adopted flexible tactics and were capable of fighting from horseback when the occasion demanded. The suggestion at Hereford is that the defence forces were told to fight from horseback when it was tactically unwise to do so. It could be speculated that the local defence levy lacked enough military professionals capable of operating effectively as cavalry; that the topography and/or conditions were wrong; that the Anglo-Saxon cavalry were outnumbered; or that the tactics were inappropriate in a defensive battle.

The description of Gruffudd 'arraying' his 'well-ordered' troops again suggests the military acumen and professionalism that he had shown throughout his career. Much of Gruffudd's force would have been mounted, as shown by their ability to closely pursue the fleeing English horsemen after the victory. Welsh troops were, like the Anglo-Saxons, accomplished warriors capable of adapting their tactics to the circumstances, and Welsh poetry of the period describes mounted men in combat. We have no evidence of archers at the battle, but medieval sources usually chose to ignore bowmen as the weapon was regarded as less honourable than the sword or spear, and was generally associated with the lower-class rabble of the army. Welsh bowmen would be famously celebrated by Gerald of Wales in the twelfth century, and it is probable that at Hereford in 1055 we should imagine their presence as part of a balanced, flexible force of cavalry, infantry and archers, whose traditional weapons – the spear, sword and bow – would have been well supplemented by the battle axes of their Viking allies. Such a hardy, well-seasoned force would have been a formidable foe for any army, let alone a local defence levy with a divided leadership. It also seems likely that, if we accept the figure of around 3,500 men under Gruffudd's command, the invaders had a strong numerical advantage. The post-battle rout describes the Anglo-Saxon force fleeing into the walled town with the Welsh hot on their heels. In the ensuing slaughter it seems unlikely that many in the defeated army could have got away, yet the number killed is estimated at just 400–500. More would have been taken captive and sold into slavery, but the army size is still unlikely to have approached the scale of that led by Gruffudd.

Little can be recreated of the battle itself, but it seems reasonable to conclude that a sharp and brutal clash was followed by Ralf's rapid retreat and the subsequent rout of his army. Even given the advantages likely to have been held by Gruffudd's force, the speed and scale of his triumph would have been unexpected, perhaps emphasising Ralf's unwise decision to keep his force mounted when an obdurate and well-defended infantry line would have provided sterner resistance. Indeed, the earl could have kept his host behind the walls of Hereford, a move that may have forced Gruffudd into a siege and perhaps have given the rest of Anglo-Saxon England time to rally to the town's aid. Hereford had been a walled town from at least the time of its earliest Anglo-Saxon occupation, excavations having revealed eighth-century fortifications.[26] We also know of a garrison there in the early tenth century under Æthelflæd, the 'Lady of the Mercians', who was renowned for her attention to fortifications in the Anglo-Saxons' ongoing struggle for dominance with the Danish settlers in England.[27] It is possible though, that the town's defences had not been maintained to a suitable standard in more recent years. In the sixteenth century John Leland said that the 'common voice' in Hereford was that the town was caught 'scant fortified with walls' when Gruffudd attacked and destroyed it.[28] The defences were then improved by Harold Godwinesson later in 1055 – the suggestion seeming to be that he did more than simply repair the damage that had been done by Gruffudd.[29] The attack from the Wye was surely unexpected, and perhaps the town's river defences were inadequate. In any case, it is clear that Gruffudd did not have to concern himself with a siege of the town as his army forced its way in during the post-battle chaos. One version of the Welsh chronicle, *Brenhinedd y Saesson*, says that the defenders of the fortification were caught while at their meal.

The savage treatment of Hereford's clergy and cathedral by the victorious army made a major impression on the Anglo-Saxon sources. The plundering of clerical wealth was commonplace in warfare between Christian leaders and could be regarded with a minimum of outrage, and the Welsh Church was certainly a target for Anglo-Saxon raids in this period.[30] While the appropriation of assets must have been expected, it is possible that the unnecessary burning of the minster and, especially, the slaughter of the seven canons, was seen as over-stepping the mark. The lives of the Welsh saints and the charters of the Book of Llandaff are replete with references to assaults on the Church and, despite problems with the reliability of the evidence, the actions can be seen as indicative of the behaviour expected of Welsh nobles in the eleventh century.[31] Offenders were always made to show contrition for their actions by grants of reparation or submission to the saints, thereby providing a justification for the particular right being claimed by the Church. A distinction can, therefore, be perceived between the nature of the assault and the expected level of reparation. The plunder of goods and provisions by armies on campaign was seen as a commonplace activity, and the troops tended to be persuaded to stop by the power of a saint's miracle and fear of his wrath.[32] The slaughter of clergy members was more unusual and unacceptable, and it was this sort of crime that was linked to rich grants of reparation.[33]

It has been suggested that blame for the level of violence involved in the attack on the clergy and cathedral of Hereford can be laid at the door of the Vikings in the victorious army.[34] The activities of separate elements in an army could be separated in this way, the *Life of St Gwynllyw* being at pains to stress that an eleventh and twelfth-century King of Gwynedd and his Welsh followers were not to blame for an assault on the saint's church that was made by their Viking allies.[35] There was also a significant Anglo-Saxon presence in Gruffudd's army at Hereford and it seems unlikely that Ælfgar would have been comfortable with the attack on the clergy and cathedral, but, as overall commander, the Welsh king must bear the responsibility for the events. The silence of the Welsh sources with regard to the treatment of the church in the town could suggest that a measure of shame was attached to the deeds perpetrated by Gruffudd's men. The misery of the Herefordshire clergy was not over, and in the aftermath of the battle the Welsh bishop Tremerig – called a deputy of Æthelstan of Hereford, perhaps suggesting that he held responsibility in Archenfield – died in a manner that would suggest that the recent events had been too much for him.[36] Æthelstan passed away the following February and these deaths – plus the fate of the next Bishop of Hereford, Leofgar, who was killed by Gruffudd in 1056 – are surely the basis for the proverb related by William of Malmesbury that no Bishop of Hereford ever lived for long.[37]

A New Enemy

Gruffudd's campaign prompted an urgent response from the Anglo-Saxon state, a reaction that the English sources were keen to portray as effective:

When the king was informed of [the events at Hereford] he ordered an army to be mustered directly from the whole of England. It assembled at Gloucester, and the king put the vigorous Earl Harold in charge of it. Zealously obeying his orders, Harold energetically pursued Gruffudd and Ælfgar, and boldly invaded the Welsh borders. He encamped beyond Straddle, but they, because they knew him to be a strong and warlike man, not daring to embark on war with him, fled into south Wales. When this was known, he dismissed the greater part of his army there, ordering the men to resist the enemy vigorously, if occasion should demand. On returning to Hereford with the rest of the host, he encircled it with a broad and deep ditch, and fortified it with gates and bars.[38]

Gruffudd was undoubtedly faced by a formidable new foe in Harold, the future King of England whose ability to mount rapid and decisive military strikes was evident throughout his career. His mustering of the 'whole of England' would suggest the gathering of a mighty army, the select levy of all England in the day having been estimated at 14,000 men.[39] Even so, the description of Harold's 'bold attack' on the invaders seems somewhat overblown. The Welsh sources merely record that, after Hereford, 'with vast spoil [Gruffudd] returned home eminently worthy.' Harold cleared the immediate danger by advancing west of Hereford into the borders of Wales, beyond the valley of the Dore, before setting up camp in Ewias. There the bulk of the army was left on a watching brief to deter another attack, while Harold himself rushed to Hereford to attend to the emergency refortification of the town. While Gruffudd is said to have retreated to 'his own land' it is questionable where that border now lay, given the significant territorial conquests he had recently made. Harold remained reluctant to engage Gruffudd, suggesting that the Welsh king had maintained the integrity of his force, a fact that reflects his power and control of his realm. It has been seen that the thirteenth-century versions of the Welsh laws suggest that a king was entitled to take his mustered army outside its locality for just six weeks, but Gruffudd's campaign greatly exceeded this duration. A source first written down in the late eleventh century by an author with connections to Gruffudd suggests that arrangements could be more flexible. The *Life of St Cadog* claims that a portion of territory belonging to the saint (known as a *cantref*) was free of all tribute to the king 'except that they had to go with thee to battle three days and nights, and, if they go with thee longer, thou shalt feed them.'[40] The date of the initial muster of Gruffudd's forces is uncertain, but Ælfgar's exile was in March, meaning that the earl is likely to have been with the Welsh king by early summer at the latest. Gruffudd then led a campaign that destroyed Gruffudd ap Rhydderch in south-east Wales before turning up the valley of the Wye against Herefordshire. The Battle of Hereford was on 24 October, a date already beyond the favoured spring and summer campaigning season. Gruffudd, though, kept his army together throughout the time it took Harold to muster 'the whole of England' at Gloucester and to advance against him into the borders.

When peace was eventually brokered between the two sides it was made at Billingsley, to the south-east of Hereford. The deal was favourable to Ælfgar who 'went back to the king, who restored his earldom to him'. This separated the earl from his Viking mercenaries, who immediately sailed from Billingsley, back down the Wye and around the Welsh coast to Chester where they were to receive the payment that had been promised to them. Gruffudd's spoils from the peace deal are not described, but it seems clear that his ongoing ambition for a kingdom of 'greater Wales' was sated by the granting of land that had formerly fallen under the sway of Anglo-Saxon Herefordshire. Many peace treaties of the day were made on the borders of opposing rulers' lands,[41] and Billingsley is situated on raised ground overlooking Hereford and the Wye. The name is remembered today in the appellation of a farm between Little Dewchurch and Holme Lacy at the north-eastern limits of Archenfield. In the eleventh century the location may still have represented something of a boundary between the English and Welsh districts of Herefordshire, making it more than a coincidence that Gruffudd chose to conclude the peace deal there.

A part of the treaty saw the diocese of Hereford cede ecclesiastical control of Ergyng to the church of Glamorgan, and the Book of Llandaff illustrates the authority exercised by Bishop Herewald in the area in the succeeding years.[42] Herewald's consecration *c.* 1056 was performed by Cynesige, the Archbishop of York, in the presence of King Edward, indicating that the English state had acquiesced in the deal. That Gruffudd was now able to exploit territories formerly under the control of the see of Hereford and that this did not please the leaders of that diocese is revealed by the events of 1056. Bishop Æthelstan of Hereford died in February of that year and was replaced by Harold's own chaplain, Leofgar.[43] Immediately after his consecration he took to war against Gruffudd and – as the wording of the *Anglo-Saxon Chronicle* leaves little doubt that Leofgar was the instigator of the renewed hostilities – it would suggest that he was unhappy with the losses that Hereford had been forced to accept in the deal made at Billingsley:

> He [Leofgar] gave up his chrism and his cross, and took his spear and his sword after his consecration as bishop, and so went campaigning against Gruffudd the Welsh king, and they killed him there and his priests with him, and Ælfnoth the sheriff and many good men with them; and the others fled. This was eight days before midsummer [16 June]. It is hard to describe the oppression and all the expeditions and the campaigning and the loss of men and horses that all the army of the English suffered, until Earl Leofric came there, and Earl Harold and Bishop Aldred, and made an agreement between them according to which Gruffudd swore oaths that he would be a loyal and faithful underking to King Edward.[44]

The battle was fought in the vicinity of Glasbury-on-Wye, an important ecclesiastical centre between Brecon and Hay-on-Wye in the Welsh sub-kingdom of Brycheiniog and close to the Herefordshire border. Glasbury is thought to have been the main location of a line of bishops known as *Clas Cynidr*.[45] A list of their names has been found on a fourteenth-century manuscript in France, where it is stated that the final bishop, Tryferyn, left for Hereford. It is likely that this was the same man named by John of Worcester as Bishop Æthelstan of Hereford's deputy, Tremerig, who died in 1055 after Gruffudd's attack on the town. One late Welsh source calls the 1056 battle at Glasbury *Gwaith Machawy*, indicating that the site can be located more precisely to the point just above the village where the stream called the Machawy – now the Bachwy – goes into the Wye.[46] It is likely that Gruffudd had maintained himself in the region since the dramatic events of the previous year. Walter Map preserves a tradition linking Gruffudd with the lake at Llangors (Llyn Syfaddan), 8 miles south of Glasbury and the

1 A rare medieval image of a Welsh king on his throne, holding a sceptre. From the law book known as Peniarth 28. *By permission of Llyfrgell Genedlaethol Cymru / The National Library of Wales*

2 Gruffudd ap Llywelyn, taken from David Powel's sixteenth-century book *A Historie of Cambria, now called Wales. By permission of Llyfrgell Genedlaethol Cymru/The National Library of Wales*

3 Looking towards the English border and Long Mountain from Hen Domen. Gruffudd's 1039 victory of Rhyd-y-groes was fought in this general area.

4 The bridge over the Severn at Buttington just outside Welshpool, looking east at the Long Mountain. The site has been suggested as a possible location for Rhyd-y-groes.

5 The River Camlad at Rhyd-y-groes on the modern England-Wales border, our favoured location for the battle site of Rhyd-y-groes (1039).

6 Carew Castle, on the tidal inlet of the River Carew. A far older and larger defended enclosure can be identified on the site and connected with the rulers of Deheubarth.

7 The magnificent stone-sculptured Carew Cross, a monument that carries an inscription to Maredudd ab Edwin, the brother of Gruffudd's rival Hywel.

8 The remains of Richard's Castle, Herefordshire. Gruffudd defeated forces from the castle in 1052, while his daughter, Nest, would later marry Osbern fitz Richard, the son of the castle's founder.

9 St Cadoc's church, Llancarfan, Vale of Glamorgan. The clerical family of Llancarfan played key roles in building the authority of the diocese of Llandaff, and Gruffudd had close connections with Herewald, Bishop of Llandaff and Magister of Llancarfan.

10 Llandaff Cathedral from the River Taff. Gruffudd seems to have worked closely with the Church as he imposed his power on south-east Wales after 1055.

11 St Mary's church, Portskewett. The village is intimately connected with the rulers of south-east Wales in the early Middle Ages and would surely have attracted Gruffudd's attention.

12 The view of Chepstow Castle from the mouth of the River Wye. Gruffudd led his fleet this way in the 1055 assault on Hereford, perhaps inspiring the construction of the castle *c.* 1067.

13 Some of the surviving medieval town walls of Hereford. There is a suggestion that the town's fortifications had been neglected before Gruffudd's 1055 attack and that Harold subsequently improved the defences.

18 The church of St Paulinus, Llangors. The Book of Llandaff lays claim to the church in a charter said to have been granted by Gruffudd.

19 On the 'Old Passage' ferry launch point at Beachley below the original Severn Bridge road crossing, looking towards Aust Cliff. Walter Map tells of a meeting between Gruffudd and Edward the Confessor at this location.

20 Twthill, Rhuddlan. The site was the location of one of Gruffudd's major administrative centres.

21 The view of the River Clwyd from Twthill. Gruffudd maintained boats on the water below his palace, giving him easy access to the sea.

22 The parish church in St Asaph lies on the River Clwyd, 3 miles upstream from Gruffudd's administrative centre at Twthill, Rhuddlan.

23 The Edwardian castle at Rhuddlan on the River Clwyd, built 300m to the north-west of Gruffudd's court at Twthill.

24 The estuary of the River Fraw from the village of Aberffraw, traditionally the chief court of the kings of Gwynedd.

25 River Usk at Caerleon. The scale and importance of the Roman port at Caerleon has been made clear by recent archaeological excavations, and the site remained easily accessible from the sea in the eleventh century and beyond.

26 The commanding view from St Woolo's Cathedral on Stow Hill to the mouth of the River Usk. Gruffudd's officials tried to control and tax boats entering the river.

27 St Woolo's Cathedral, Stow Hill, Newport. The *Life of St Gwynllyw* tells of an attack on the church by Harold, and it is possible that this was the first act in his final campaign against Gruffudd.

28 Gruffudd's final weeks were spent in the remote and hostile wilds of Snowdonia.

29 The undated earthworks known as Domen Castell, Llanfechain. A local tradition suggests that Gruffudd's sons were killed in this vicinity, in the 1069 Battle of Mechain.

30 Sixteenth-century stained glass window from Llangadwaladr church, Anglesey. The image is of Cadwaladr the Blessed (d. 682), the man who Geoffrey of Monmouth portrays as the last in his legendary line of the kings of Britain, Geoffrey claiming that his death led the 'Britons' to take on the name 'Welsh'.

site of a traditional court of the kings of Brycheiniog.[47] Such an administrative centre and natural resource may have played a key role in keeping Gruffudd's sizeable military presence well provided for through the winter and into the 1056 campaigning season.[48]

Recognition and Consolidation

Leofgar's disastrous attack was repulsed with brutal and merciless ease by Gruffudd, reflecting his established dominance over local Anglo-Saxon levies even when the Welsh ranks were not bolstered by the presence of Viking mercenaries. The peace deal that followed Gruffudd's victory saw Edward recognise the Welshman's position as an independent underking within the British Isles. This has been regarded by some as a reduction in the Welsh leader's status which had been forced upon him, and Frank Barlow claims that Gruffudd 'was constrained to acknowledge that he was an under-king'.[49] But such an interpretation bears no resemblance to the political realities that had forced the English magnates to make the truce. Gruffudd had smashed England's border defences and made significant territorial conquests in 1055, and after the treaty that was made at Billingsley that year he had remained in the vicinity to ensure that the terms were honoured. Leofgar's 1056 attempt to reverse Gruffudd's gains had ended in disaster at Glasbury, leaving the Welsh king in an even more domineering position. Harold would have been a formidable presence among the English magnates subsequently sent to make terms with Gruffudd, but Aldred, the Bishop of Worcester, had only been back in the country for a short time after diplomatic missions on the continent and had been handed emergency control of Hereford after Leofgar's demise. Earl Leofric of Mercia's loyalties would have been open to question due to the tensions between his family and Harold's, and given the fact that his only known child and heir, Ælfgar, was Gruffudd's ally.

That Gruffudd was not compelled to attend King Edward's courts nor to serve in his armies indicates that this was not a punitive settlement imposed upon him. Even more telling is the fact that Edward conceded to Gruffudd 'all the lands beyond the river called Dee'.[50] Domesday Book shows that, with the exception of a narrow strip along the Dee estuary, Gruffudd was in control of all the territory between the rivers Dee and Clwyd. Offa's Dyke runs through the middle of this borderland in north Wales, revealing that Gruffudd had acquired land that had been in English hands from the eighth century until his day. John Edward Lloyd noted that English westward expansion had continued after the building of the dyke, with settlements like Edderton, Forden, Thornbury, Woodliston and Hopton in the region of Montgomery, and, further south, the likes of Waterdine, Weston, Pilleth, Radnor, Burlingjobb, Kington and a group of villages on the north bank of the Wye around Eardisley. Such areas, and many others along the entire length of the Wales-England border, are recorded as 'waste' in Domesday Book, many yielding no dues to the English exchequer as late as 1086. This can be used to indicate the extent of Gruffudd's conquests, some of which may have been made before 1056 but which were confirmed by the treaty of that year. The change in political master for the borderland was accompanied by peasant colonisation, meaning that the area was reclaimed for the Welsh language, law and custom.[51] The ecclesiastical boundaries of St Asaph may also have been established at this time, and it is notable that until 1920 the see contained a number of parishes from across the English side of the border.[52]

Gruffudd's territorial and ecclesiastical gains in Herefordshire have been noted, to which Walter Map adds a revealing tale of an otherwise unknown meeting between Gruffudd and King Edward.[53] Although the encounter cannot be historically verified, it is known that Edward regularly held court at Gloucester and Map is likely to have got the tale from traditions in that part of the world. The story furthermore fits with the political events of c. 1056, with Edward giving the royal seal of approval to the agreement that had been made between Gruffudd and Harold, Leofric and Aldred. Map pictured the two kings facing off on opposite banks of the Severn, with Gruffudd at Beachley near Chepstow and Edward at Aust Cliff in Gloucestershire (the site of the original Severn Bridge road crossing). This was the location of an ancient ferry crossing known as the 'Old Passage' and the western side had been left in Welsh hands when Offa's Dyke was constructed as the border in the eighth century. By the eleventh century though, Beachley was usually in English hands, making Map's association of the land with Gruffudd significant whether the meeting with Edward happened or not.

After years of striving for power, Gruffudd finally seemed to have become content and secure in the position he had won within a greater Wales. His reign entered a period of calm, save for a notable anomaly in 1058. The events of that year are shrouded in obscurity in all the source material, but hidden behind the confusion could be a sequence of events as dramatic as the invasion of Herefordshire in 1055. The catalyst was the death in 1057 of the two earls whose lands were immediately adjacent to Gruffudd's: Leofric of Mercia (sometime in autumn 1057) and Ralf of Herefordshire (December 1057). Ælfgar succeeded his father in Mercia but had to give up his claims to East Anglia, and the lands that this freed up allowed the creation of two new earldoms for Harold's younger brothers, Gyrth and Leofwine. Ralf's son and heir was merely a child, and his Herefordshire lands were merged into Harold's earldom of Wessex, thus further strengthening the position of the Godwines within England and isolating Mercia. This led Ælfgar to turn back to his established ally Gruffudd, and it is at this time that we should date the marriage of the Welsh king to Ælfgar's daughter, Ealdgyth.

Ælfgar's cultivation of his alliance with Gruffudd served him well in 1058. John of Worcester gives the clearest account, although one lacking in his usual detail: 'Ælfgar, earl of the Mercians, was outlawed by King Edward a second time, but with the help of Gruffudd, King of the Welsh, and the support of the Norwegian fleet, which joined him unexpectedly, he quickly recovered his earldom by force.'[54] The *Anglo-Saxon Chronicle* seems determined to be vague about the events: 'In this year Earl Ælfgar was banished but he came back forthwith by violence through Gruffudd's help. And a naval force came from Norway. It is tedious to relate fully how things went.'[55] The Welsh chronicle does not even mention Ælfgar, concentrating on the role of Gruffudd and the fleet from Norway: 'Magnus, son of Harold, king of Germany [*sic*], came to England, and he ravaged the kingdoms of the Saxons, with Gruffudd, king of the Britons, as a leader and a help to him.'[56] Magnus, the leader of the Viking fleet, was the son of the King of Norway, Harold Hardrada, the man who would have such a dramatic impact on the events of 1066. Magnus himself would succeed his father as king, and his arrival on the scene in 1058 would have been with a major military force. Irish sources suggest that Magnus was making a bid for the kingdom of England itself, but while we should not rule out this possibility, it is more likely that his expedition was concerned with his ambitions in the Isle of Man and the western isles. The combination of his troops with those of Gruffudd and Ælfgar can only point to the gathering of a formidable army, and the suggestion in the source material seems to be that the Welsh king was the dominant partner. While we can glean little more of events from the sources, it is clear that the English state was soon impelled to return Ælfgar to his former position. The apparent sense of shame in the Anglo-Saxon sources would suggest that Gruffudd and Magnus profited with great spoil from their ravaging. It is likely that they were paid off to prevent further attacks without having to face an armed challenge, a shameful situation for the Anglo-Saxons that would revive painful memories of previous Danegelds.

Thanks to his strategic sense and aggressive policies since 1039, Gruffudd had become king of all Wales and a major player on the wider stage of Britain and the isles. His conquests, which had forged a greater Wales, were moreover recognised by the English Crown. Gruffudd's borders were secure thanks to his alliance with Ælfgar to the east and his ability to manipulate and direct the Viking threat to his exposed coastlines. He began to cast his web of alliances deeper into the English polity, with his daughter Nest marrying Osbern fitz Richard, one of the Norman lords established on the Herefordshire border by Edward the Confessor.[57] Gruffudd was at the apogee of his power and in a stronger position than any other Welsh king. The question remaining was whether he could consolidate his rule.

Notes

1. *ASC* (C, D and E), pp.116, 120–1.
2. See F. Barlow, *Edward the Confessor* (London, 1989), p.94.
3. *Ibid.*, p.110.
4. Stenton, *Anglo-Saxon*, pp.569–70.
5. *ASC* (E), p.122.
6. *ASC* (C & D), pp.122–3.
7. *ASC* (D), p.122. David Walker suggested that it was Gruffudd ap Rhydderch who was responsible for this raid because the 'attack was made rather far

south for it to have come from Powys or Gwynedd'; see his 'Note', p.87. But if the strike had come from the south it is likely to have fallen closer to Hereford rather than at Leominster in northern Herefordshire. Moreover, John of Worcester's account of the 1052 raid refers to Gruffudd as King of Wales, the phrase he consistently applies to Gruffudd ap Llywelyn rather than Gruffudd ap Rhydderch, who he associates with just the south.

8. Christopher Lewis has argued that the term 'waste' in this context referred to geld that had been remitted in certain border districts ceded to Gruffudd ap Llywelyn in the 1050s prior to the recovery by the Crown in the 1060s. See his 'English and Norman Government and Lordship in the Welsh Borders, 1039–87' (unpublished D.Phil thesis, Oxford, 1985), pp.129–66.

9. Stenton, *Anglo-Saxon*, p.417.

10. Swegn always maintained an independence of action from his father and brothers and is not thought to have enjoyed good relations with Harold. A tradition even suggests that Swegn was not Godwine's son, but rather an illegitimate child of Cnut's. See F. Barlow, *The Godwins* (Harlow, 2002), pp.53–5.

11. See F.C. Suppe, 'Who was Rhys Sais? Some comments on Anglo-Welsh relations before 1066', *The Haskins Society Journal*, 7 (1995), 63–73; see also F.C. Suppe, 'Interpreter families and Anglo-Welsh relations in the Shropshire-Powys marches in the twelfth century', *ANS*, 30 (2007), 196–212.

12. JW, p.577.

13. *HW*, II, pp.364–5; idem, 'Wales and the coming', 134; Walker, 'Note', 89–90; Maund, 'Ælfgar', p.183.

14. See S. Davies, *Welsh Military*, pp.50–1.

15. *Law*, p.124; see also p.41. This issue is complicated by the fact that the surviving Welsh laws were not written down until the early thirteenth century. There could also be variations in different parts of the country.

16. See S. Davies, *Welsh Military*, p.53.

17. See pp.63, 82–3, 93.

18. Domesday Book, 'Herefordshire', folio 181a.

19. *Brut* (Pen. 20), s.a. 1056.

20. Even today, many of the place names in the area betray their Welsh origin. For example, Much Dewchurch and Little Dewchurch are derived from Dewi Sant (Saint David).

21. See Stenton, *Anglo-Saxon*, pp.340–1; H.R. Loyn, 'Wales and England in the tenth century: The context of the Athelstan charters', *WHR*, 10 (1980–81), 283–301.

22. D.P. Kirby, 'Hywel Dda: Anglophil', *WHR*, 8 (1976–77), 1–13. For the original text, see I. Williams (ed.), *Armes Prydein: The Prophecy of Britain*, Eng. vers. R. Bromwich (Dublin, 1972).

23. *ASC* (C), p.131; JW, p.579.

24. *Brut* (Pen. 20), s.a. 1056.

25. JW, 1055.

26. I.W. Walker, *Mercia and the Origins of England* (Stroud, 2000), p.172.

27. See Stenton, *Anglo-Saxon*, pp.326–7, 336.

28. L. Toulmin Smith (ed.), *The Itinerary of John Leland in or about the years 1535–1543*, vol. II (London, 1964), p.66.

29. See p.62. For archaeological evidence of Harold's refortification of Hereford, see P. Rahtz, 'Hereford', *Current Archaeology*, 9 (1968), 242–6; R. Shoesmith, 'Hereford', *Current Archaeology*, 24 (1971), 256–8.

30. See, for example, *Brut* (RBH), s.a. 978; *Vitae*, pp.111–13, 187, 229–31. For discussion of Harold's attack on the church of St Gwynllyw in the 1060s, see pp.109–11.

31. For more on the Book of Llandaff, see p.82.

32. See, for example, *Vitae*, pp.187, 219, 225, 299; *Text of the Book of Llan Dav*, pp.264–5, 272–3.

33. See, for example, *ibid.*, pp.125, 217–18, 249, 257, 259–60, 261–2, 267, 271–2.

34. Charles, *Old Norse*, p.46.

35. *Vitae*, p.185. The king was Gruffudd ap Cynan, and it could also be suggested that his Hiberno-Scandinavian allies were responsible for the severity of his ravaging of Powys in 1075 when 'he spared not even the churches', but in this example the Welsh source material glories in its hero's savagery; see *Gruffudd ap Cynan*, p.69.

36. It is likely that Tremerig can be connected to the Welsh religious centre at Glasbury-on-Wye, the home of a line of bishops known as *Clas Cynidr* who have associations with churches in Brycheiniog (Glasbury, Llan-y-wern, Aberyscir, Cantref, Llanddetty, Llangynidr) and Herefordshire (Bredwardine, Kenderchurch); for more on this, see p.64.

37. William of Malmesbury, *De Gestis Pontificum Anglorum*, ed. N.E.S.A. Hamilton (London, 1870), p.304; see also the account of the burning of Hereford, p.300.

38. JW, 1055, p.579.

39. Barlow, *Edward*, p.171.

40. *Vitae*, p.81; for the possible connection of this work of hagiography to Gruffudd, see pp.94–5.

41. See, for example, the importance of Rhyd Chwima (Montgomery) as noted in J.B. Smith, *Llywelyn ap Gruffudd, Prince of Wales* (Cardiff, 1998), pp.139–86.

42. LL, pp.546ff. For discussion, see C.N.L. Brooke, *The Church and the Welsh Border in the Central Middle Ages* (Woodbridge, 1986), pp.10–11, 14, 92–4.

43. Bishops were charged with significant responsibilities for local defence, especially on the Welsh border. See Barlow, *Edward*, pp.173, 198.

44. *ASC* (C), 1056. *HW*, II, p.368 locates the battle in the Machawy valley above Glasbury.

45. See D. Petts, *The Early Medieval Church in Wales* (Stroud, 2009), p.170; see also above, fn. – 36 [p.70].

46. See Lloyd, 'Wales and the coming', 135, fn 3. The source can be found in 'O oes GwrthernGwrtheneu' in J. Rhys and J.G. Evans, *The Text of the Bruts from the Red Book of Hergest* (Oxford, 1890), p.405.

47. Map, pp.186–9.

48. For more on this, see pp.78, 85–6.

49. Barlow, *Edward*, p.137; see also W. Davies, *Wales in the Early Middle Ages* (Leicester, 1982), p.114.

50. Domesday Book, 'Cheshire', folio 263a. For discussion, see Lloyd, 'Wales and the coming', 122–79; Stenton, *Anglo-Saxon*, p.574.

51. See *Age*, p.26.

52. See Brooke, *Church and the Welsh Border*, pp.12–13. Brooke says that the formal drawing of the diocesan boundaries are more likely to have been associated with Madog ap Maredudd in the mid-twelfth century, but notes that these bounds were 'strikingly close' to the conquests that had been made by Gruffudd a century earlier.

53. For the text detailing this meeting and further discussion, see pp.90–1.

54. JW, 1058.

55. *ASC*, 1058.

56. *Brut* (RBH), s.a. 1058.

57. This marriage cannot be securely dated and it is possible that it occurred after Gruffudd's fall in 1063. Even then, though, it would suggest the degree to which Gruffudd and his family had been accepted as major figures amongst the nobility of Britain. Osbern was the son of Richard fitz Scrob, the founder of Richard's Castle and a likely leader among the forces that Gruffudd defeated in 1052.

4

KING OF WALES

RUFFUDD HAD ESTABLISHED Wales as a united and independent state for the only time in the country's long history, but the nature of the sources available make it difficult to define the character and extent of his dominion. This has led some historians to query the legitimacy of his claims to be a great king. Wendy Davies, for example, says: 'Only in some sense was he ruler, for Gruffudd spent most of his reign campaigning to establish and maintain his own position: he had little time for "rule" in any real sense of the word.'[1] Such a summary dismissal of Gruffudd's abilities and of his achievements as King of Wales is unwarranted. It has been seen that he had a powerbase in Powys before 1039 and that he had enjoyed unchallenged recognition as King of Powys and Gwynedd since that year, giving him a long period to secure and develop his rule. He also held dominion over at least a part of Deheubarth from 1039 and, after long campaigning to win uncontested rule over the whole of that region, his position had been secure there since sometime in the period 1048–52. In 1055 Gruffudd brought south-east Wales into his kingdom, along with border areas of Herefordshire; the latter move the culmination of a long campaign to expand the whole eastern frontier of his realm into lands that had been in the hands of the Anglo-Saxons for centuries. From 1057–63 the Welsh chronicle is all but silent on internal affairs, suggesting a time of peace and stability under Gruffudd's rule, the king later being remembered as a 'shield' and 'defender' of the country and its people. The only recorded Viking activity in Wales in this period came when Gruffudd directed mercenary forces or allies to further his own ambitions, a tactic that helped him to win his border conquests. The Welsh king appears in control of relations with England after 1055 and, following the ill-documented events of 1058, Gruffudd's border conquests and acknowledged position as King of Wales, as recognised by the treaty with Edward, were secure. The new stability provided by the devolution of power on the England-Wales border was shown when the sees of Worcester and Hereford were left vacant in 1058 when Bishop Gldred went on pilgrimage to Jerusalem. It is possible that Earl Harold went to Rome in the same year, while a number of prominent Anglo-Saxon nobles made the journey to the Eternal City in 1061.[2] These years of peace gave Gruffudd time to extend the sort of dominion that he held in his heartlands of Powys and Gwynedd over the rest of his conquered kingdom.

The *Maerdrefi*

The thirteenth-century Welsh law texts provide a model of the sort of society that supported a Welsh king in the Middle Ages.[3] The picture is idealised and cannot be pinned to a particular era; elements of the laws are far earlier than the thirteenth century, laws were also subject to manipulation over the years and there were significant regional variations. However, the general picture of society is supported by evidence suggested by other surviving sources that date from post-Roman times through to the later Middle Ages. The evidence portrays a society that would have been recognisable throughout western Europe in the Middle Ages, with a noble minority of the military class being supported by the servile majority of the population who were tied to the land that they worked. The laws outline an organisation that divided kingdoms into 'hundreds' (W. *cantrefi*), each of which was split into two commotes. A commote was divided into twelve manors, with four townships in each manor, while there were two other townships in each commote, known as *maerdrefi*, that were reserved exclusively for the use of the king. Out of the twelve manors in each commote, one was to support the king's reeve, another his chancellor, and four others were worked by the king's bondmen. The remaining six fell to the control of the leading nobles of the land (W. *uchelwyr*). The king exploited his domains while on circuit (W. *cylch*) with his household, taking his dues in the form of food and shelter, although there also seems to have been the capacity for commuted renders, certainly by the thirteenth century. While the idealised, large-scale legal model can be questioned and would have been open to innumerable variations in the real world, the existence throughout Wales of small, nucleated settlements ('townships') that were used as administrative units and exploited by kings on their tours through their lands is clear.[4]

Gruffudd's rule was pinned to his major administrative centres, his *maerdrefi*, that were situated throughout the country. The most extensive studies of such Welsh royal courts in the period have been conducted in Gwynedd, one of the areas where Gruffudd was most secure and where he held longest dominion.[5] Finding actual evidence of these *maerdrefi* is extremely problematical though, as the best sites were re-used through-out the ages. The Norman invaders after 1066 tended to build their early earthworks in Gwynedd on top of the Welsh *maerdrefi*, although later Welsh and Anglo-Norman stone castles were more usually constructed on fresh, more strategic sites that would then usurp the administrative role of the old *maerdref*. In general terms, it seems that the *maerdrefi* were not associated with strong fortifications and that accessibility was more important in choosing their location. This is not to suggest that Welsh lords were incapable of con-structing fortifications, or that static defence was totally neglected. The wall of a king's court had its gate guarded at night by a watchman, whose house behind the entrance was strong enough to hold prisoners.[6] The Welsh laws outline a king's right to a man with an axe from every villein townland to work on his fortifications, the resources of the bondmen thus being uti-lised to work on the defences of the *maerdref*.[7] Such centres were associated with the native rulers of the land and when they were fortified they were described with ancient Welsh terms, including *caer* and *din*. Smaller, heavily defended private fortifications had no part within the Welsh kingdoms, and when the term *castell* ('castle') was used it was associated with alien intru-sions into the country. Welsh nobility below the rank of king either lacked the resources to construct such structures, or were restrained from doing so by royal command. Welsh kings did not use such last-ditch redoubts because, ultimately, they had to defend their dominion and its resources in the field. It also made little sense in Wales to concentrate resources in one centre when the country had a neighbour like England. The Anglo-Saxon state was able to concentrate formidable resources against Wales, but major, royal expeditions were rare and tended to be short lived. When faced with such an overwhelming force a typical Welsh leader would be foolish to present a static target, however formidable its defences, and would instead take to the wilds of the country and harry invaders with guerrilla tactics.[8]

Given the itinerant nature of a Welsh king's rule it is incongruous to talk of Gruffudd having a 'capital', but he developed a site at Twthill, Rhuddlan, into a major court, and perhaps this even took on the characteristics of his main administrative centre. As with Hereford, an association with Rhuddlan would suit Gruffudd both practically and for the purposes of propaganda. Rhuddlan had been an important strategic location throughout the preceding centuries, with the river below Twthill the best fordable spot on the River Clwyd for many miles along its marshy estuary. The Anglo-Saxons and Welsh had vied for control of north-east Wales in the centuries before Gruffudd, and we know of a clash of arms in the area in 796, the so-called Battle of Morfa Rhuddlan. Welsh legend has associated this great Anglo-Saxon victory with the completion of Offa's Dyke, and it has also been suggested that Offa's death in 796 was in some way connected to the conflict. The Anglo-Saxons penetrated the area in the early tenth century, and there are references to their fortified burh at 'Cledemutha' (Rhuddlan) in the period 921–*c.* 950.[9] This was a large, rectangular enclosure of approximately 30 hectares, a site that is comparable to contemporary burhs in Wessex. A tradition survives that Rhuddlan was used by Gruffudd's father, Llywelyn ap Seisyll, as a royal residence,[10] and it is the site that is most closely associated with Gruffudd himself in English sources.[11] This Anglo-Saxon evidence also tells us that Gruffudd had a naval force at Rhuddlan that gave him access to the open sea from his court, a capability that would have been vital to his wider aims.[12] It has been suggested that the importance of controlling river traffic was the primary reason for the Anglo-Saxon construction of their tenth-century burh,[13] and in the late twelfth century Gerald of Wales described how the River Clwyd 'flows by Rhuddlan Castle and so comes to the sea'.[14]

The importance of Gruffudd's alliance with Ælfgar is clear, and developing a significant court at Rhuddlan would have helped his communications with the Mercian earl. Domesday Book supplies rare, additional evidence for the sort of logistical support that would be provided for a major site like Rhuddlan from the king's other resources. Seventeen miles to the south-east, Gruffudd possessed another, smaller court (W. *llys*) that controlled the manor of Bistre. The king is said to have had one plough in the lord-ship while his men had six, and when Gruffudd visited the court 'every plough paid him 200 loaves, a barrel of beer and a vessel of butter'.[15] The important church of St Asaph, the centre of the diocese of that name, stands 3 miles south of Rhuddlan on the River Clwyd. Legend suggests that the see was founded in the sixth century, but its origins can only be securely traced to the middle of the twelfth century.[16] A St David's document of 1145 claims that one of their bishops consecrated a man named Melan to St Asaph *c.* 1070, the only known reference to an eleventh-century bishop at the church. The problematic nature of this evidence means that little more can be said, but Gruffudd would surely have found it useful to have a strong ecclesiastical official close to his court at Rhuddlan. The strategic value of the location was further demonstrated after Gruffudd's death as the Norman invader Robert of Rhuddlan built a motte-and-bailey castle *c.* 1073 on the site of the former king's court. The twelfth-century Welsh prince Owain Gwynedd would later develop his own castle there, with Gerald of Wales spending a night in the fortification on his journey through Wales in 1188 and describing 'a fine castle on the River Clwyd'.[17] It was the setting for Llywelyn ap Gruffudd's submission to Edward I in the first war of conquest in 1277, and soon afterwards the English king began the construction of the imposing stone castle that dominates the town to this day, built on a green field site just 300m to the north-west of Twthill.

Elsewhere in Gwynedd, acknowledged pre-1100 centres that are secular and of high status include Degannwy, Dinas Emrys and Aberffraw. David Longley has also noted the 'striking correspondence' between early earth-work castles and locations that are believed to be older *maerdref* sites.[18] It is not known whether these fortifications were built by the Welsh or the Normans, but it seems certain that the administrative roles of the *maerdref* were performed from these locations. The sites include Rhuddlan, Degannwy, Bangor, Aberlleiniog and Caernarfon, with Denbigh and Abergwyngregyn other possibilities. With the exception of Dinas Emrys and Denbigh, all of these sites would have had easy access to the sea.

Gruffudd made use of royal centres throughout the rest of the country as he expanded his power in Wales and, as in Gwynedd, the majority of known *maerdrefi* locations have later castles in the vicinity, and also tend to have ecclesiastical centres nearby.

We do not know the date when the sub-kingdom of Brycheiniog came under Gruffudd's sway; he was active in the area in 1055–56, but it is possible that this had been one of the earliest territories to fall to his power. Likely *maerdref* sites in Brycheiniog include Talgarth/Bronllys, Aberhonddu (Brecon) and Hay-on-Wye.[19] It is also notable that Walter Map preserves a tradition associating Gruffudd with Llangors, a village 6 miles to the east of Brecon.[20] This was a traditional *llys* of the kings of Brycheiniog, and a ninth-century artificial island constructed by the local ruler on the large freshwater lake there is the only known example of a Welsh crannog, a type of settlement that was common in Scotland and Ireland.[21] The crannog was burnt in 916 following a raid by Æthelflæd, the 'Lady of the Mercians'. The artificial island was not reoccupied, but the village remained an important administrative centre into the Anglo-Norman period. As has been noted, Gruffudd was in the vicinity of Llangors with a large army in the period 1055–56, winning a battle at the important ecclesiastical centre of Glasbury, 8 miles to the north, and it is possible that he had used the rich natural resources from the land and lake to keep his men supplied.[22] The Book of Llandaff has a number of charters wherein the Church lays claim to the village and its wealth, particularly noting its fish and fisheries for eels.[23] Gerald of Wales described the natural abundance of Brycheiniog and Llangors in the twelfth century:

> This area produces a great amount of corn ... There is ample pasture and plenty of woodland, the first full of cattle, the second teeming with wild animals. There is no lack of freshwater fish, both in the Usk and the Wye. Salmon and trout are fished from these rivers, but the Wye has more salmon and the Usk more trout. In winter salmon are in season in the Wye, but in summer they abound in the Usk. The Wye is particularly rich in grapling, an excellent fish which some call umber ... [the lake in Llangors], a broad expanse of water which is very well known, supplies plenty of pike, perch, excellent trout, trench and mud-loving eels for the local inhabitants.[24]

Locating the *maerdrefi* used by Gruffudd in his original powerbase of Powys is more troublesome. Perhaps the most promising site for further archaeological investigation can be found next to Brycheiniog in Elfael, the southernmost *cantref* of Powys. Cwrt Llechryd in Llanelwedd, a little to the north of Builth Wells, is an earthwork that is thought to have been constructed between the ninth and tenth centuries, and carbon dating has given a date of occupation of *c.* 750–1040. This site bears comparison to others like Mathrafal (near Welshpool) and Plas-yn-Dinas (near Llansantffraid-ym-Mechain), where Norman motte-and-bailey castles are surrounded by rectangular earthwork enclosures. It had been thought that these were traditional Welsh centres, that the earthworks pre-dated the Norman works and were fortifications with Roman and Anglo-Saxon influences. Comparison was made between these high-status sites and others nearby that are thought to have been of Mercian origin, including Buttington, New Radnor, Old Mills Moat and Forden Gaer.[25] However, excavation work at Mathrafal found no pre-Norman evidence, revealing that the earthworks represented the bounds of a medieval estate that post-dated the castle.[26] The tradition that Mathrafal is one of the three ancient capitals of Wales along with Aberffraw (Gwynedd) and Dinefwr (Deheubarth) comes from the later Middle Ages and is unreliable, nevertheless the surviving site was an important fortification used by both Anglo-Norman and Welsh lords in the twelfth and thirteenth centuries. There are also the remains of an earlier fortification about a mile to the north, and it is possible that this was the *maerdref* in the eleventh century. Without further archaeological investigation it is difficult to say more, but it should be noted that a battle was fought in the vicinity of Plas-yn-Dinas in 1069 between Gruffudd's sons and brothers, who were contending to succeed him as King of Wales.[27] Also, the example of Cledemutha/Rhuddlan indicates that sites like Buttington, New Radnor and Forden Gaer could have been utilised by Gruffudd after his border conquests, even if the ultimate provenance of these fortifications was Anglo-Saxon.

The *maerdref* sites were focal points as Gruffudd progressed his war for control of south Wales after 1039. His first recorded strike in Deheubarth was against the monastery of Llanbadarn Fawr. This is close to Aberystwyth, an area that had known fortification since at least the Iron Age and that

would be castellated by the Normans in the early twelfth century. It has
been seen that Gruffudd's protracted showdown with Hywel ab Edwin cen-
tred on Carmarthen, a town that would be associated with a Norman castle
as early as 1094 and where the surviving Roman fortifications remained
imposing. The 1041 battle between the two Welsh kings was at Pencader,
10 miles north of Carmarthen and the site chosen for an Anglo-Norman
castle in 1145. The fact that Gruffudd seized Hywel's wife after the battle
could suggest that he had caught his rival by surprise at one of his courts.
Hywel held out against Gruffudd in the deep south-west in Dyfed, and
likely *maerdref* sites there include Narberth, Tenby and Carew. Narberth is
named as the chief court of the rulers of Dyfed in the prose tales of the
Mabinogi. There are a number of earthworks in the area, while the first reference to a Norman castle in Narberth is in 1116.[28] The surviving stone
castle at Tenby is on the site of an Iron Age fortification, and the town's
Welsh name, *Dinbych*, means 'small fortress'. The site is referred to as the fort
(W. *caer*) and stronghold (W. *dinas*) of a Welsh king in the ninth-century poem
'The Praise of Tenby'.[29] Even more intriguing is Carew, 6 miles to the west
of Tenby and now the site of an imposing stone castle. The ancient Welsh
name means 'the fortifications' (W. *caerau*) and excavations have revealed a
defended enclosure that encompasses a far greater area than that covered
by the later castle. This could be dated anytime between the Iron Age and
1066, and is composed of at least five parallel lines of rock-cut ditches,
while the northern and western approaches to the site find protection from
the tidal inlet of the River Carew.[30] Nearby stands the magnificent stone-
sculptured Carew Cross, a monument that carries an inscription to Maredudd
ab Edwin, Hywel's brother, who had held joint rule of Deheubarth with
him until his death at the hands of Gruffudd's cousins in 1035. The origins
of the fortification and cross pre-date the time of Maredudd and Hywel
and are strongly indicative of an ancient royal tradition in the area that had
been inherited by the brothers. Gruffudd is likely to have taken over these
traditions – and the administrative functions of sites like Narberth, Tenby
and Carew – after his final victory over Hywel in 1044.

Perhaps the most intriguing potential *maerdref* to consider in south-east
Wales is Portskewett, a coastal site on the Severn estuary in southern Gwent,
4 miles south-west of Chepstow and close to the western end of the new

Severn Bridge road crossing. The area has Iron Age connections and is just 2 miles south-east of the important Roman civilian centre of Caerwent. Welsh literature of the early medieval period names Portskewett as a major port and tradition associates it with Welsh royalty: the semi-legendary sixth-century king of Gwent, Caradog Freichfras.[31] A charter in the Book of Llandaff lays claim to the area on behalf of the Church, noting its fisheries 'and with free approach of ships at the mouth of Pwll Meurig'.[32] In 1065 Harold, seeking to roll back the conquests that Gruffudd had made on the Wales-England border and advance into Welsh territory, built a hunting lodge at Portskewett. The location was used as an administrative centre, as Harold: 'got together many goods [there] and thought of having King Edward there for hunting.'[33] This was an unacceptable insult to the native ruler, Gruffudd ap Rhydderch's son Caradog, who had emerged as ruler of Gwent. He led an attack on the site and slaughtered the English workmen, and Portskewett became part of the region that would prove to be Caradog's main sphere of activity. Such a site would have attracted Gruffudd ap Llywelyn's attention after his defeat of Gruffudd ap Rhydderch in 1055, and it is notable that Walter Map portrays the northern king operating boats from Beachley, just a few miles from Portskewett, before his meeting with Edward (c. 1056).[34]

The other major Roman site in the area, Caerleon, is another administrative centre that would have been utilised in south-east Wales. Gerald of Wales noted the impressive Roman walls and remains in the twelfth century, while the earliest reference to a Norman motte-and-bailey castle at the site comes in 1086. This was almost certainly the location of one of Caradog's courts that was taken over after his death in 1081. It is another site that Gruffudd could have reached with his fleet, as seen from Gerald's description: 'Caerleon is beautifully situated on the bank of the River Usk. When the tide comes in, ships sail right up to the city. It is surrounded by woods and meadows.'[35] There is a reference to a nephew and officer of Gruffudd's, Rhiryd ab Ifor, rushing to the mouth of the Usk to enforce trading tariffs and it could be speculated that he was based at Caerleon.[36]

Administration, Officers and Resources

The landed dominion that Gruffudd held had a strong legal underpinning, with professional ministers to implement his policies. Charters of the king survive in the Book of Llandaff, a work compiled by Norman clerics in the 1120s. The scribes put together their work at Llandaff, making creative use of Welsh traditions in the form of saints' lives, charters, papal bulls and relics in order to support the claims of their struggling diocese in boundary disputes with Hereford and St David's. Contained within the tome are the lives of the three supposed founding saints and bishops of Llandaff, along with 158 charters that claim to be dated from the sixth to the end of the eleventh century.[37] The problems faced in using this evidence are legion, but the chronology that ties its version of events with the people mentioned and the attached witness lists is generally reliable. The book helps establish the presence of a charter tradition in different monastic centres throughout south Wales before the coming of the Normans, and its evidence gives examples of the expected conduct of Welsh noblemen and churchmen of the day.

In the book, Gruffudd is named as 'King of all Wales' when he appears as chief lay witness for the consecration of Bishop Herewald of Llandaff, and also on a charter confirming the see 'in all its property, including that in Brycheiniog'.[38] This was from the period after 1055 when the northern king had killed Gruffudd ap Rhydderch – giving him control of Llandaff and the rest of south-east Wales – and at a time when he is known to have been active in Brycheiniog. Gruffudd's confirmation of rights would have been key to his securing the allegiance of the new bishop, one of the most important men in his recently conquered territory. Meurig ap Hywel, the King of Glamorgan, is also named as a witness at the consecration, ranked third among the laity after Gruffudd and his son, suggesting that Meurig had been accommodated as a client ruler within Gruffudd's kingdom of Wales. On the charter, the important Glamorgan nobleman Caradog ap Rhiwallon – a man considered powerful enough to have made his own land grant to Llandaff – is the third lay witness after Gruffudd and his son. It is possible that the church of Llandaff had opposed the Gwent-based Gruffudd ap Rhydderch in his conflict with Meurig in the 1040s, and that Herewald, Meurig and Caradog were allies of Gruffudd ap Llywelyn in 1055. It is also possible that property claimed by the church in Glamorgan had been damaged in the war of 1055 and that this was a reparation grant to regain clerical favour, a repeat of the policy that had seen Gruffudd ap Llywelyn win over the clergy of Deheubarth following his ravaging of Llanbadarn Fawr in 1039. Gruffudd was instrumental in extending the power of the Glamorgan church further. Herewald's subsequent consecration of estate churches in Ergyng are described as occurring 'in the time of Edward, King of the English, and Gruffudd, King of the Welsh'.[39] Gruffudd's conquests and new status in the borderlands had given the Glamorgan church the opportunity to expand its own sphere of influence eastwards at the expense of the see of Hereford, events that seem likely to have been linked to the Battle of Glasbury in 1056.[40]

That Gruffudd was able to expand his direct power into at least certain sections of south-east Wales is revealed by the fact that his poet, Berddig, was granted land in Gwent on terms that were free from all dues. Berddig was politically active in the south-east; he is referred to in Domesday Book and appears as a witness on Llandaff charters.[41] The estates given to Berddig are likely to have been freed up by the slaying or removal of the men who had supported Gruffudd ap Rhydderch, thus allowing Gruffudd ap Llywelyn to dispense a king's most sought-after form of largesse – conquered land. Later princes of Gwynedd would use poets as propagandists and politicians. Meilyr Brydydd, for example, served Gruffudd ap Cynan as an emissary in the early twelfth century, and in 1223 Einion ap Gwalchmai was one of the men appointed by Llywelyn ab Iorwerth to define the political and geographical boundaries between the warring petty princes of Deheubarth.[42] The fact that Berddig continued to hold land and power in the south-east after Gruffudd's death indicates that his knowledge and service were of value to the new rulers of the area. Other alien officers may have been introduced to the south-east by Gruffudd. The *Life of St Gwynllyw* refers to 'Ednywain of Gwynedd' who is described as 'a most intimate friend' of Caradog ap Gruffudd, Gruffudd ap Llywelyn's successor in south-east Wales.[43] The continued faith placed in the north Welshman was unfounded as Ednywain is said to have broken into Gwynllyw's church and stolen from there, whereupon he was judged at a court presided over by Caradog and Bishop Herewald.

The court poet is just one of the officers described in the Welsh laws. This corpus indicates that a cadre of professional personnel would surround the king and be responsible for the administration of his realm. The model for this organisation can be traced back to at least the time of Hywel Dda in the mid-tenth century[44] and the presence of such officers has been used to suggest that Gruffudd's court was 'directly related to the ideal Carolingian household'.[45] The *History of Gruffydd ap Cynan* – a mid- to late twelfth-century work that purports to describe events of *c.* 1055–1137 – refers to a nobleman called Llywarch Olbwch, who was said to have been the 'most trusted chamberlain and treasurer of Gruffudd ap Llywelyn'. It has been noted that Llywarch was the name recorded by Walter Map as being a nephew of Gruffudd's who had escaped the king's family bloodletting in his rise to power.[46] The *Life of St Gwynllyw* refers to another nephew of Gruffudd's – the previously mentioned Rhiryd ab Ifor – who is depicted enforcing the king's trading tariffs in south-east Wales in the 1060s, again in the land that had been conquered from Gruffudd ap Rhydderch.[47] If these sources are correct in naming Llywarch and Rhiryd as Gruffudd's nephews, it is unlikely that they were the sons of his only securely identified siblings, his half-brothers Bleddyn and Rhiwallon. The known offspring of those two men were of the next generation and proved active in late eleventh- and twelfth-century Powys where they were well recorded by the genealogists. Walter Map uniquely claims that Gruffudd had a sister and, if this is correct, she may have been a full sister, the product of Angharad's first marriage, to Llywelyn ap Seisyll. If Gruffudd's sister had sons they would have been men of the age and rank expected to fill high office in the king's regime. Other family members are likely to have been used in Gruffudd's administration; the diplomatic work between Mercia and Wales undertaken by Rhys Sais has already been indicated, and it is possible that he, too, was related to the king.

There are surviving hints that Gruffudd pushed the limits of the legal resources at his disposal in order to gain maximum revenue for his ambitious policies. Although Gruffudd was clearly a domineering king, the sources also suggest that, ultimately, he had to rely on the judgements of his legal experts and the nobles of the realm. This can be inferred from Walter Map's story of Gruffudd's jealousy with regard to his 'very beautiful wife'.

The king is said to have been enraged on hearing that a young nobleman had dreamt of having an affair with the queen, and to have demanded retribution. Gruffudd threatened the youth with torture and death and threw him into jail, refusing the 'custom' claimed by his clan of offering themselves as security. The matter was finally turned over to a man described as pre-eminent in such dealings, who declared:

> We must follow the laws of our land, and can by no means annul what our fathers ordained and what has been established by long use. Let us then follow them and not produce anything new until a public decree directs us to the contrary. It has been promulgated in our oldest laws that he who outraged the consort of the King of Wales should pay 1,000 kine to the king and go free and unharmed. With regard to the wives of princes, and every class of magnates in like manner, a penalty was appointed according to the rank of each, with a certain number specified. This man is accused of dreaming that he abused the queen and does not deny the charge. Had the offence confessed been real, it is certain that 1,000 kine would have to be paid. In respect that it is a dream, we adjudge that this young man shall set 1,000 kine in the king's sight on the bank of the lake in Behthen [Llangors], in a row in the sunlight, that the reflection of each may be seen in the water, and that the reflections shall belong to the king, and the kine to him who owned them before, inasmuch as a dream is the reflection of the truth. This decision was approved by all and ordered to be put in execution, in spite of the angry protests of [Gruffudd].[48]

Perhaps we can read into this story the memory of Gruffudd's hunger for resources that saw him push his rights to their limits, however dubious the grounds. Writing in the later twelfth century, Gerald of Wales remembered Gruffudd as a man who 'for so long had oppressed all Wales by his tyranny'.[49] Gruffudd is not held up in later tradition as a model of ideal Welsh kingship in the manner of Rhodri Mawr or Hywel Dda. It is notable that Gruffudd's half-brother and successor, Bleddyn, is known to later tradition as a law reformer. This perhaps suggests that such readjustment was needed after the reign of Gruffudd, but it can also be explained by the fact that Bleddyn founded a dynasty, with descendants who would seek to promote his legacy. The connection to Llangors in Map's story seems significant, given Gruffudd's extended presence with a large military force in the area from the winter of 1055 and into 1056. The exploitation of customs and dues for military necessities was characteristic of Llywelyn ap Gruffudd in the late thirteenth century and caused the erosion of his support within Wales before the Edwardian Conquest.[50] In Gruffudd's case, it is possible that such squeezing of resources only occurred at the height of his border wars with England. It must also be noted that he had far greater resources to call on than Llywelyn ap Gruffudd, including the richest lowlands of Wales and the borders.

To consider other resources that the king might rely upon, it has been seen that Walter Map called a youthful Gruffudd 'a most crafty and formidable raider of others' goods' and his long series of successful wars would have brought plentiful plunder into his coffers.[51] His ravaging campaigns were many, but amongst those referred to are the raid on Llanbadarn Fawr in 1039 and the wasting of Ystrad Tywi and Dyfed in 1047. It could be suggested that passages in the lives of the Welsh saints allude to the demands made by Gruffudd on lands in the south-east and to his ravaging of the area.[52] These were, of course, territories that Gruffudd would ultimately rule and develop, so such harrying was not a sustainable policy in the long term. Gruffudd's raids across the rich English border would have been even more valuable, with notable successes in 1052, 1055 and 1058. As the Welsh chronicle says, after ravaging Hereford in 1055 'with vast spoil [Gruffudd] returned home eminently worthy'. The *Anglo-Saxon Chronicle* is more fulsome, describing how Gruffudd 'took many captives, despoiled and burned the city, and returned enriched with a lavish quantity of booty'. The latter quote suggests an important element in Gruffudd's plunder that is hidden to us in other sources – his slave raiding. It has been seen that bondmen formed an important element in Wales' society and economy, while Viking raiders had long targeted slaves as one of their primary booties in raids on Wales and the rest of Britain. In Ireland, the slave trade was central to the growth of royal power as profits allowed for the consolidation of resources and the payment of large armies, and it is likely that Gruffudd used the money raised from the sale of slaves to Ireland to fund his wider ambitions.[53]

Such spoils of war were not the king's only revenue however, as Gruffudd profited from the rich realm that he had won. In the most general of terms, the mid-eleventh century in western Europe was a time of improving climate, rising population, economic growth and the accumulation of wealth in the hands of landowners.[54] The *Life of St Gwynllyw* describes Gruffudd's officials enforcing the toll that was levied at the mouth of the Usk against English merchants who refused to pay, and the *Book of Llandaff* suggests that a similar charge was imposed at Portskewett. Gerald of Wales' description of the rich lands of Brycheiniog has been noted. He wrote similar praise of other wealthy lowland territories such as Pembrokeshire; lands that formed part of Gruffudd's domain but had fallen under Anglo-Norman and Flemish control by the twelfth century.[55] Gerald also described lucrative silver works in Tegeingl, close to Gruffudd's court at Rhuddlan: 'We passed through a district where there is a rich vein of silver and successful mining works and where, by delving deep, "They penetrate the very bowels of the earth".'[56] That Gruffudd's attempt to marshal such wealth from his kingdom was successful is illustrated by references in the Welsh chronicle that mention his 'innumerable treasures of gold and silver and gems and purple raiment' and the 'many feasts and delights' enjoyed at his court.[57] Even English sources were impressed by the 'girded chests' and 'royal pomp' found at Gruffudd's palace in Rhuddlan, and, perhaps even more significantly, by the impressive fleet that he was able to maintain.[58]

Naval Strategy

The strategic importance of sea power to any ruler of Wales is obvious from a look at the map, with the country being bordered by open water to north, south and west, and many of the rich lowlands situated around the coastal shelf. Despite this, Gruffudd is the only native king who presents us with evidence to indicate that he maintained an independent navy and maritime strategy. There are suggestions that other major Welsh leaders of the early Middle Ages may have had ambitions in this area, and it is notable that most of these are associated with Gwynedd. The importance of Welsh ships is clear in the early prose tales *Culhwch and Olwen* and in the *Four Branches of the Mabinogi*; this would at least suggest that there was nothing incongruous in the idea of Welsh rulers maintaining naval capability. It should be noted, however, that references to famous seafarers in the *Triads* generally seem to allude to leaders based outside of Wales.[59] Tradition suggests that Cunedda, the semi-legendary founder of the first dynasty of Gwynedd, came to Wales by sea from the north and settled on Anglesey, with Aberffraw later acknowledged as the main seat of power for his descendants. In the sixth century, Gildas acknowledged Maelgwn Gwynedd as the most powerful British ruler of his day, and he gave the great king the title of 'the island dragon'. In the next century, Cadwallon ap Cadfan was driven from Gwynedd by Edwin of Northumbria, but the fact that he was able to escape to Ireland before returning with enough force to defeat Edwin would suggest that he enjoyed some sort of naval capability. Tradition also links Merfyn Frych and the second dynasty of Gwynedd with arrival by sea from the north (in the early ninth century) and with a base in Aberffraw. Rhodri Mawr enjoyed notable military success against Viking raiders, while his son, Anarawd, is likely to have used sea power in his wide-ranging campaigns across Wales.

After Anarawd's death there was a notable rise in Hiberno-Scandinavian interference in Wales and a dearth of references to native naval capability. This is understandable when consideration is made of Wales' neighbours and rivals in the Irish Sea region. Viking raiders from Ireland, the Isle of Man and further afield were renowned masters of the sea, and the threat posed by such marauders troubled the greatest kingdoms of early medieval Europe. Wales' formidable land neighbour to the east, England, was also a force to be reckoned with on the water. The Anglo-Saxon state's ever-growing ambition in the region was illustrated in 973 when King Edgar was symbolically rowed on the Dee by eight kings drawn from Wales, Scotland, northern England and the western isles.[60] It is possible that the rise of such forces contributed to Wales' increasing insularity at this time, with overseas trade declining as native rulers were denied access to the shipping lanes.[61]

Gruffudd would struggle to compete against such established naval powers, and it is clear that his first known campaign in 1039 was conducted on land. After the Battle of Rhyd-y-groes he headed west across the mountains of mid-Wales to Llanbadarn, before descending on Hywel ab Edwin in southern Deheubarth. In Gruffudd's long-running campaign against Hywel, it was the southern king's ability to marshal the support of ships from Ireland that kept him in with a chance of success. A fleet from Ireland was the core element of Hywel's army in the decisive battle at the mouth of the Tywi in 1044, and his suggested *maerdref* sites at Tenby and Carew both had easy access to the sea. The obscure reference to Gruffudd's capture at the hands of the 'Gentiles of Dublin' in 1042 also needs to be considered in this context, and Hiberno-Scandinavian raiders of Deheubarth were an obstacle to Gruffudd's ambitions until the foundering of one of their fleets in 1052. After that date, Gruffudd made positive use of alien sea forces in his hugely successful campaigns of 1055 and 1058, with the role played by naval power in the slaying of Gruffudd ap Rhydderch and the destruction of Hereford having been highlighted.

This still fails to suggest an independent naval strategy from Gruffudd as he relied on allied or mercenary fleets, but now, with all the resources of Wales behind him, he worked on developing his own fleet. Walter Map describes Gruffudd and his leading nobles operating boats at Aust Cliff on the Severn before his meeting with Edward the Confessor, and we have suggested that the Welsh ships would have been based at Portskewett.[62] Most significantly, John of Worcester, the *Anglo-Saxon Chronicle* and the anonymous *Life of King Edward* (*Vita Ædwardi Regis*) all refer to Gruffudd's significant naval presence on the River Clwyd at Rhuddlan in 1063.[63] The context of the references indicate that the Welsh king had built this fleet in competition to that of his English enemies. Gruffudd is depicted sailing from his court at Rhuddlan at short notice, the rich trappings of his flagship detailed thus: 'A prow and stern of solid gold, cast by smith's assiduous skill'.[64] Later in that year, Harold and Tostig felt the need to co-ordinate ground and sea forces for a campaign against Gruffudd, again suggesting the ability of their enemy on both land and water.

Given the problems faced in maintaining good land communications in mountainous Wales, Gruffudd's sea power was vital as he tried to weld his disparate kingdom together. Sailing from his court at Rhuddlan, the Welsh king would have had easy access to his ally Ælfgar in Chester, and to coastal *maerdref* sites in Gwynedd such as Degannwy, Abergwyngregyn, Bangor, Aberlleiniog, Aberffraw and Caernarfon. Moving south, locations like Aberystwyth, Carew and Tenby would have been open to him from the sea, while he could sail up waterways like the Tywi towards Carmarthen.

The *Life of St Gwynllyw* has a reference to Gruffudd's officers controlling naval traffic at the mouth of the Usk, and the river provided access to the royal centre at Caerleon.[65] The damage that Gruffudd did along the Wye and up to Hereford in 1055 has been detailed, and Portskewett would have served as a natural base for such an enterprise. Independent naval power allowed Gruffudd to project his might and was a stand-out, perhaps unique, aspect of his reign when compared to the other native kings of Wales.

The Trappings of a King

Gruffudd also used more subtle means to project his power, authority and dignity as a king worthy of respect on the European stage. His flagship's 'prow and stern of solid gold, cast by smith's assiduous skill' needs to be seen in this context as it was clearly an object of note, beauty and value. One version of the Welsh chronicle refers to Gruffudd as 'the golden torqued king',[66] the torque being a high-status item of a previous age that retained an anachronistic relevance in praise poetry of the Middle Ages.[67] Other elements of his image and attire projected Gruffudd's position. In the previously mentioned story from the *History of Gruffydd ap Cynan*, the hero of the work meets a kinswoman of his named Tangwystl, who was the wife of Gruffudd ap Llywelyn's treasurer and chamberlain, Llywarch. Tangwystl presents Gruffudd ap Cynan with 'the thinnest and finest shirt and tunic made from the mantle of King Gruffudd, son of King Llywelyn, son of Seisyll.'[68] This reveals that the dynasty of Gruffudd ap Cynan was keen to be associated with the trappings of a king as powerful as Gruffudd ap Llywelyn, even though there may have been other good reasons for the line to distance themselves from his memory, as will be considered later.[69] Gruffudd's mantle is also described by Walter Map in the story of the Welsh king's meeting with Edward the Confessor, indicating that it was an object of some fame:

> In the midst of [Gruffudd's] works of wickedness there is one thing he is recorded to have done nobly and courteously. In his time he was so oppressive and obnoxious to his neighbours that it became necessary for Edward,

then king of England, either to use entreaty on behalf of his subjects, or take up arms in their defence. Ambassadors were sent from both sides and then they negotiated from opposite banks of the Severn, Edward being at Aust Cliff, [Gruffudd] at Beachley. The nobles went to and fro between them in boats, and after many exchanges of messages, the question was long debated which of them ought to cross over to the other. It was a difficult crossing owing to the roughness of the water, but that was not the ground of the dispute. [Gruffudd] alleged his precedence, Edward his equality: [Gruffudd] took the ground that his people had gained all England, with Cornwall, Scotland, and Wales, from the giants, and affirmed himself to be their heir in a direct line: Edward argued that his ancestors had got the land from its conquerors. After a great deal of quarrelsome contention Edward got in a boat and set off to [Gruffudd]. At that point the Severn is a mile broad. [Gruffudd] seeing him and recognising him cast off his state mantle – for he had prepared himself for a public appearance – went into the water up to his breast and throwing his arms lovingly about the boat, said: 'Wisest of kings, your modesty has vanquished my pride, your wisdom has triumphed over my foolishness. The neck which I foolishly stiffened against you you shall mount and so enter the territory which your mildness has today made your own.' And taking him on his shoulders he seated him upon his mantle, and then with joined hands did him homage. This was an admirable beginning of peace, but, after the Welsh manner, it was only kept till they felt able to do mischief.[70]

Although Map portrays Gruffudd as morally inferior to the pious Edward, and despite the fact that the Welshman eventually submits to the English ruler, the mutual status of the two as kings is emphasised. Gruffudd's casting off of the mantle that he had worn to 'prepare for public appearance' should be seen in the terms outlined by Robin Stacey. She says that 'clothing and politics are intimately intertwined' and that in the Welsh prose tales of the day 'changes in garb often accompany or denote transitions in the social status or moral standing of prominent characters'.[71] The importance of such a garment can be compared to the mantle of King Arthur, which receives numerous mentions in Welsh literary tradition and is named in the *Triads* as one of the '13 Treasures of the Island of Britain'.

91

Art and Literature

There are indications that Gruffudd was a patron of the arts, or at least that the arts flourished under the peace that followed his conquests. The most common form of support that was indulged in by Welsh nobles was the patronage of bards, who would sing praise poetry to their lord in his courts. As has been seen, the senior bards would be officers of court and a part of a king's administration of his realm. The liberal grants received by Gruffudd's poet Berddig in the conquered lands of south-east Wales have been noted, but it is likely that many more received the king's largesse on a smaller scale. The younger poets would be expected to live cheek-by-jowl with the king's household, travelling with it and fighting with it, the laws making provision for such a role with the office of *bardd teulu*. A class of itinerant bards existed, travelling around the courts of Wales where they would, quite literally, sing for their suppers. It is notable, though, that there is no surviving poem directed in praise of Gruffudd himself. Given the positive nature of references to Gruffudd in other native literary sources, the absence of praise poetry to him seems unlikely to indicate that he was unpopular amongst the artistic classes, nor that he failed in his duty of patronage to the bards. It could be because poems to Gruffudd were simply lost in the succeeding centuries, but it is more likely that later princes of Wales chose not to support panegyric works to him for dynastic reasons. The poems of the day were transmitted orally and would not be written down for many years to come. To survive they would need to be sung in the courts of Welsh noblemen, but, as will be seen, all the major dynasties of Wales that followed Gruffudd would have good reason for wanting to forget him, either through hatred, or through shame at the role they had played in his final months.[72]

The favour that both Gruffudd and his father Llywelyn found with the St David's-based native chronicle has been noted, and it is likely that this was as a result of their patronage of the church in Deheubarth when they held dominion over that part of Wales. Gruffudd ap Llywelyn had ravaged Llanbadarn Fawr at the start of his southern campaign in 1039, but he then had many years to rectify the damage and to win over the clerical class of south Wales.[73] The head of the most prominent Welsh clerical and cultural family in Deheubarth in the eleventh century was named Sulien (1011–91).

His home and library were at Llanbadarn Fawr and he was Bishop of St David's towards the end of his life, suggesting that he would have played a role in the lauding of the reputations of Llywelyn and of his son Gruffudd. Both men are described as 'king of the Britons' in the Welsh chronicle, a title that was reserved for only the greatest of Welsh leaders. Llywelyn is lauded as:

> King of Gwynedd and the supreme and most praiseworthy king of all Britain. And in his time, as the old men were wont to say, the whole land from the one sea to the other was fruitful in men and in every kind of wealth so that there was no-one in want nor anyone in need within his territory; and there was not one township empty or desolate.[74]

Gruffudd is described thus: 'He, from his beginning to the end, pursued the Saxons and the other Gentiles and slaughtered and destroyed them, and defeated them in a great number of battles.'[75] At the end of his reign, Gruffudd was glorified as the 'head and shield and defender to the Britons',[76] and even over fifty years after his death the Welsh chronicle remembered him, with the 1116 entry describing Bleddyn ap Cynfyn as 'the foremost of the Britons after Gruffudd ap Llywelyn'.[77]

The king also found favour from clerics in the conquered lands of south-east Wales, the Book of Llandaff describing him in imperial terms as *rege Grifido monarchia britonum prepollente* ('King Gruffudd, sole and pre-eminent ruler of the British').[78] It has been seen that Gruffudd was the chief lay witness at the appointment of Bishop Herewald of Llandaff and that he helped the Glamorgan church to press claims to authority in Ergyng. Herewald, who died in 1104, must have been a young man at the time of his consecration and he is likely to have owed a lot to the backing of the king. The new bishop may have been fired with a reforming zeal and it is possible that he introduced archdeacons to the Glamorgan church, although this may just be a later claim of the Book of Llandaff.[79] The church's scribes also outline an elaborate charter of Gruffudd's, confirming the see in all its rights, a piece of work that lauds the king's power and largesse. If the details of the charter can be regarded as indicative of Gruffudd's character, they suggest that such munificence was unusual in the king, but hint that he had at least a basic level of conventional piety:

[God] inspired the stony heart (a disease of the body seizing him) of Gruffudd, King of Britain, and as I may say, of all Wales from one extremity to the other, and warmed it with the fervour of the Holy Spirit. The king therefore observing that his power was as the flower of the field, and his flesh as ashes, endeavoured to obtain for transitory substance, a kingdom flourishing without decay, and heavenly joy without grief and sorrow and removed from all want, and accepting himself the yoke of penance, and repenting of what he had done contrary to the divine precepts, promised amendment of himself, by fasting and prayer, and almsgiving, and the bestowing by him of various precious metals to God, and to poor widows and orphans. And not degenerating from the nobility, piety and liberality of his predecessors, but imitating and excelling them in energy and bravery as well against the barbarous English on the one part, who always fled on seeing his face in battle, as against the western Irish, who always put to flight, and against the natives of the country, who according to their usual custom were fond of war, and against the Danish seamen, and against the inhabitants of the Orkney islands, who always turned their backs in flight, and peaceably confirmed treaties agreeably to his wishes, he gave up to the Church of Llandaff of Peter the apostle, and of the holy confessors Dubricius, Teilo and Oudoceus, all the territories of its diocese from the mouth of the Taratyr on the banks of the Wye to the banks of the Towy; and moreover its lands of Llandeilo Fawr, and Penaly with many other churches, and all their lands, and with those many in the district of Brecknock, which are held without the diocese, in that of St David's, as is shown in the chirograph, and with all their privileges as were in the best manner observed in the time of his predecessors quit and free from all regal service, except only daily prayer for the souls of the Kings and Princes of Britain, and the grant was confirmed with placing his hands upon the four gospels, and ratified in the hand of the Bishop, and before all his people, on the day of the nativity of our Lord, at Ystumgwy, and with the offering of the village of Penrhos in the hand of the Bishop, and all the Bishops of Llandaff forever.[80]

The years of Gruffudd's dominance were close to the time of the formulation of some of the earliest and most influential 'lives' of the Welsh saints, notably those of St Cadog (first composed *c.* 1072–1104) and St Gwynllyw (first composed late in the second half of the eleventh century).[81] Wendy

Davies stresses the recurrent theme in such hagiography of the inroads made by northern kings into south Wales and says that the growth in claims to church immunities was a response to such threats to their independence.[82] Gwynllyw and Cadog flourished in sixth-century Wales, but Davies believes that the real events behind the later legends were the attacks of Anarawd ap Rhodri Mawr of Gwynedd on south Wales in the late ninth century. Gruffudd's campaigns in the south would have been far fresher in the memory though, and there are other reasons to connect him with the stories. Lifris of Llancarfan, the author of the *Life of St Cadog*, was the son of Bishop Herewald of Llandaff, an adherent and probable ally of Gruffudd's who enjoyed the king's grants of rights to his church. Both the lives of St Cadog and of St Gwynllyw are associated with the scriptorium of the clerical family of Llandaff/Llancarfan and deal with relations between south-east Wales and the neighbouring kingdom of Brycheiniog. It has been noted that Gruffudd was active across both these areas in 1055–56, having based himself in Brycheiniog with significant forces that would have needed many victuals.[83]

Gruffudd's reign is likely to have played a role in encouraging the formulation of Wales' great literary prose tales of the early Middle Ages, the *Four Branches of the Mabinogi*. These were amongst the earliest works of the later eleven-tale collection that came to be known as *The Mabinogion*; the 'four branches' individually called *Pwyll, Branwen, Manawydan* and *Math*. The possible harnessing of this material in the reign of Gruffudd has been seen as an attempt 'on the part of a native of Dyfed to unite the stories of his own province with those of Gwynedd and Gwent when all three provinces were under one ruler'.[84] The most recent edition of the work suggests that the 'four branches' were brought together in the period *c.* 1060–1120.[85] It has already been noted that the late twelfth- or early thirteenth-century tale *The Dream of Rhonabwy* used Rhyd-y-groes, the location of one of Gruffudd's greatest victories, as the setting for a scene where contemporary warriors were compared unfavourably with Welsh leaders of the past.[86]

Walter Map's story of Gruffudd's meeting with Edward the Confessor suggests that the Welsh king used the most famous legends associated with his land to build his own mythology. The reference to Gruffudd claiming superiority over Edward and dominion over all Britain because his ancestors 'in a direct line' had conquered the giants indicates that the Welsh king had tapped into the rich vein of material that would be so effectively exploited by Geoffrey of Monmouth in the twelfth century with his *History of the Kings of Britain*. Stories of King Arthur and of the expected return of a *Mab Darogan* ('Son of Destiny') would have suited Gruffudd's propaganda as he sought to unite Wales and to reclaim borderland from the Anglo-Saxon state. Arthur makes regular appearances in the lives of both Cadog and Gwynllyw, and in *Culhwch and Olwen*, and it seems reasonable to speculate that Gruffudd was a patron of such legends, with his support helping to pass on the traditions that would be recorded by Geoffrey and would then have a huge impact on the literature of medieval Europe.

Family and the Succession

The fact that Gruffudd did not found a dynasty has tended to be used by historians to denigrate his achievements, but it seems that he had attempted to put such plans in place. We know that Gruffudd had at least two partners. He claimed the unnamed wife of Hywel ab Edwin as his own after the Battle of Pencadair in 1041, then married Ælfgar's daughter Ealdgyth *c.* 1057, thereby cementing his alliance with the Mercian earl. It is possible that Gruffudd's first known partner had died by this time, but we cannot rule out the possibility that she had been put away, or that Gruffudd retained two (or more) wives.[87] One genealogical tract claims that Gruffudd was married to Ceinfryd, the daughter of Rhirid Mawr, and that they had a son named Cynan.[88] If she existed, Ceinfryd may have been the wife that Gruffudd took from Hywel, or she may have been another woman, but we have no other references to her, nor to Cynan. It has been noted that Walter Map claimed that Gruffudd 'had a very beautiful wife, whom he loved more ardently than she loved him, for which reason he gave his whole energies to spying on her chastity, and burning with suspicion and jealousy, cared for nothing but that none other should touch her'.[89] This could refer to any of Gruffudd's partners, but the twelfth-century Anglo-Norman writers Orderic Vitalis and William of Jumièges described Ealdgyth as 'beautiful' and she would seem to be the woman most likely to attract Map's attention.[90] As the granddaughter

of the famous Lady Godiva, Ealdgyth also had something of a family tradition to uphold for allurement and for raising the jealousy of husbands.

Welsh leaders of the Middle Ages often sired sons by a variety of partners, and the laws of partible inheritance meant that all could be regarded
as legitimate heirs.[91] We do not know how many offspring Gruffudd had,
but the Welsh chronicle's mention of the death of Owain ap Gruffudd in
1059 is almost certainly a reference to a son of the king. The notice is the
chronicle's only entry regarding domestic events in the period 1057–63 as
the country enjoyed the peace and stability that Gruffudd had won. Owain
ap Gruffudd is otherwise unknown in our sources, but for the chronicle
to mention his death indicates that it was an event worthy of notice. With
Gruffudd having taken the wife of Hywel ab Edwin in 1041, it can be speculated that Owain was the fruit of their union, and by 1059 he could have
been around 17 years of age and a likely successor to the king's throne. This
is suggested by the possibility that he was the 'Owine' who witnessed four
Mercian charters in conjunction with Earl Leofric and his son, Gruffudd's
ally Ælfgar.[92] It is even possible that Owain's death was related to Gruffudd's
recent marriage to Ealdgyth. If Owain was seen as the heir apparent, he
could have been concerned at the possibility of being elbowed aside by the
children of his new step-mother and plotted a rebellion, or he could have
been moved against by powerful rival factions at court.

The Welsh king had at least two other sons, Maredudd and Idwal, and
they are known to have worked in co-operation after their father's death.
It is likely that Maredudd was the elder and a man who was groomed for
power by Gruffudd. He is named as a witness to Bishop Herewald's consecration and to a charter in the Book of Llandaff; Gruffudd's ability to
wield power in the south-east means that these references must be dated
to the period 1055–63. Maredudd's position of eminence is suggested by
the fact that his name appears second amongst the lay witnesses. On each
he is named after his father, appearing before King Meurig ap Hywel of
Glamorgan at the consecration and ahead of the important nobleman
Caradog ap Rhiwallon on the charter.[93] Maredudd and Idwal are then
named as 'the sons of Gruffudd' in 1069 when the pair fell in battle, fighting
as allies to try to win a part of the patrimony in the political chaos that followed the death of Gruffudd ap Llywelyn.[94] For the brothers to have been

of military age in 1069 suggests that they, like Owain, were the children of the woman that Gruffudd had taken in 1041. If Owain was the eldest son from that marriage, then Maredudd and Idwal are likely to have been minors in 1059, meaning that the death of Owain would have opened up a power vacuum. Gruffudd's only known daughter, Nest, may have been from his marriage to Ealdgyth;[95] if so, she is the only child that can be identified from their union, and, in any case, their offspring would need many years to reach maturity.[96] Such a situation would have awakened the ambitions of the other native noble lines in Wales, men of royal blood who had served Gruffudd out of a mixture of loyalty, self-interest and compulsion. The great king was beginning to age and his conquests were at an end, meaning that gifts of land and riches to his leading followers were in shorter supply. Such a political climate would prove a breeding ground for treachery.

Notes

1. W. Davies, *Wales*, p.106.
2. *ASC* (D), p.135; JW, p.587; *Vita Ædwardi Regis*, ed. and trans. F. Barlow (1962), p.33; see also Barlow, *Edward*, pp.209–10.
3. For discussion, see G.R.J. Jones, 'The tribal system in Wales: A re-assessment in the light of settlement studies', *WHR*, 1 (1960–63), 111–32; *idem*, 'The distribution of bond settlements in north-west Wales', *WHR*, 2 (1964–65), 19–36; *idem*, 'Post Roman Wales', in H.P.R. Finberg (ed.), *The Agrarian History of England and Wales*, I, ii (Cambridge, 1972), pp.281–382; *idem*, 'Multiple estates and early settlement', in P.H. Sawyer (ed.), *Medieval Settlement* (London, 1976), pp.15–40.
4. See, for example, T.M. Charles-Edwards, 'Early medieval kingship in the British Isles', in S. Bassett (ed.), *The Origins of Anglo-Saxon Kingdoms* (Leicester, 1989), pp.28–39; D. Longley, 'The royal courts of the Welsh princes of Gwynedd, AD 400–1283', in N. Edwards (ed.), *Landscape and Settlement in Medieval Wales* (Oxford, 1997), pp.41–54; J.K. Knight, 'Welsh fortifications of the first millennium AD', *Château Gaillard*, 16 (1992), 277–84.
5. See Longley, 'Royal Courts'; N. Edwards, 'Landscape and Settlement in Medieval Wales: An Introduction', in *ibid.*, 1–11; p.3; N. Johnstone, 'Llys and Maerdref: The royal courts of the princes of Gwynedd', *Studia Celtica*, 34 (2000), 167–210.

6. See *HW*, I, p.314.

7. *Law*, p.125.

8. For further discussion of Welsh fortifications in the period, see S. Davies, *Welsh Military*, pp.190–217.

9. F.T. Wainwright, 'Cledemutha', *EHR*, 65 (1950), 203–12; H. Miles, 'Rhuddlan', *Current Archaeology*, 3 (1972), 245–8; J. Manley, 'The late Saxon settlement of Cledemutha (Rhuddlan), Clwyd', in M.L. Faull (ed.), *Studies in Late Anglo-Saxon Settlement* (Oxford, 1984), p.55; *idem*, 'Rhuddlan', *Current Archaeology*, 7 (1982), 304–7; N. Edwards and A. Lane (eds), *Early Medieval Settlements in Wales, AD 400–1100* (Bangor and Cardiff, 1988), pp.110–13; R.R. Davies, *Conquest*, pp.30–1.

10. W. Warrington, *The History of Wales*, 4th edn (Brecon, 1823), p.311; S. Lewis, *A Topographical Dictionary of Wales*, II, 4th edn (London, 1849), p.352.

11. See the references to Gruffudd's palace at Rhuddlan in *ASC* (D), p.136 and JW, p.593.

12. For further discussion see pp.87–90.

13. See I.W. Walker, *Mercia and the Making of England* (Stroud, 2000), pp.107, 126.

14. *Description*, p.230.

15. Domesday Book, 'Cheshire' folio 269b; see also H.P.R. Finberg, *The Agrarian History of England and Wales*, I (Cambridge, 1972), p.308.

16. If it is accepted that there was a church at St Asaph in the early Middle Ages it is likely to have been on the site of the parish church next to the River Clwyd rather than where the cathedral is located at the top of the hill.

17. *Journey*, p.196.

18. Longley, 'Royal Courts', p.45. The names and general locations of over twenty *maerdref* sites in Gwynedd are known, but it should be noted that the evidence is from documents of the thirteenth and fourteenth centuries.

19. Walter Map told a story of a Welsh youth from the 'fort' at Hay-on-Wye, although it is not clear whether he was dealing with an incident he imagined occurring before or after the Norman conquest of the area; *Map*, p.201.

20. *Ibid.*, pp.186–9.

21. See E. Campbell and A. Lane, 'Llangorse: A tenth-century royal crannog in Wales', *Antiquity*, 63 (1989), 675–81; E. Campbell, A. Lane and M. Redknap, 'Llangorse crannog', *Archaeology in Wales*, 30 (1990), 62–3.

22. See pp.64–5.

23. *LL*, pp.388–9, 499–500, 523.

24. *Journey*, p.93; Gerald adds that in winter the lake is covered in water fowl; *ibid.*, p.94.

25. For this interpretation, see C.R. Musson and C.J. Spurgeon, 'Cwrt Llechryd, Llanelwedd: An unusual moated site in central Powys', *Medieval Archaeology*, 32 (1988), 97–109.

26. C.J. Arnold, J.W. Huggett and H. Pryce, 'Excavations at Mathrafal, Powys, 1989', *The Montgomeryshire Collections*, 83 (1995), 59–74; also C.J. Arnold and J.W. Huggett, 'Pre-Norman rectangular earthworks in mid-Wales', *Medieval Archaeology*, 39 (1995), 171–4.

27. See p.130. The village of Llanfechain is also in the near vicinity of Plas-yn-Dinas. The motte-and-bailey of Domen Castell in the village has been dated to sometime between the eleventh and thirteenth centuries. The Norman St Garmon's church is situated within a circular churchyard, suggesting its origins as a pre-Christian religious site. Roman coins have been found near the village's bridge over the River Cain; the waterway's name is a fitting title if it can be connected to the family disputes that followed Gruffudd's fall.

28. See N. Ludlow, 'The castle and lordship of Narberth', *The Journal of the Pembrokeshire Historical Society*, 12 (2003), 5–43.

29. *Beginnings*, pp.155–76.

30. See D. Austin, *Carew Castle Archaeological Report, 1992 Season Interim Report* (Lampeter, 1993).

31. Gerald of Wales chose to measure the length of Wales from the mouth of the River Gwygir in Anglesey to Portskewett, estimating the length of the journey between the two points at eight days; *Description*, p.220.

32. *LL*, p.495.

33. *ASC* (C), s.a. 1063.

34. See pp.90–1.

35. *Journey*, p.115. Writing earlier in the twelfth century, Geoffrey of Monmouth described the Caerleon that he knew as he told of a supposed court of King Arthur's that was held there: '[Situated] on the River Usk, not far from the Severn Sea, in a most pleasant position, and being richer in material wealth than other townships, this city was eminently suitable for such a ceremony. The river which I have named flowed by it on one side, and up this the kings and princes who were to come from across the sea could be carried

in a fleet of ships'; see Geoffrey of Monmouth, *The History of the Kings of Britain*, ed. and trans. L. Thorpe (Harmondsworth, 1968), p.226. Recent excavations at Caerleon have pointed to the size and importance of the Roman port at the site.

36. See pp.110, 112.

37. See W. Davies, *The Llandaff Charters* (Aberystwyth, 1979).

38. *LL*, p.536. For the full text of this charter, see pp.93–4 . Llandaff rights are also confirmed in the rebellious lands of Ystrad Tywi that had proved so troublesome to Gruffudd, and at a site as far west as Penally, just outside Tenby. The origins of the diocese of Llandaff cannot be securely traced until the Norman period, but we have followed the argument of Wendy Davies in contending that it is possible to refer to bishops of Llandaff from at least the time of the supposed accession of Herewald's father, Joseph, in 1022; see W. Davies, 'The Consecration of the Bishops of Llandaff in the tenth and eleventh centuries', *BBCS*, 26 (1974–75), 64–6. For the opposing view that the origins of Llandaff cannot be set this early and that Herewald was brought in by Gruffudd as a young and ambitious cleric from Ergyng with close English affiliations, see Brooke, *The Church and the Welsh Border*, pp.10–11, 14, 92–4.

39. *LL*, pp.546ff.

40. See pp.84, 110, 112.

41. Domesday Book, 'Gloucestershire', folio 162a; *LL*, pp.541, 544, 545.

42. See R. Turvey, *Llywelyn the Great* (Llandysul, 2007), p.125.

43. *Vitae*, pp.187–9.

44. See D. Jenkins, 'The lawbooks and their relation', in T.M. Charles-Edwards, M.E. Owen and P. Russell (eds), *The Welsh King and his Court* (Cardiff, 2000), pp.10–28.

45. Crouch, *Image*, p.286; see also D.B. Walters, 'Comparative aspects of the tractates on the laws of court', *The Welsh King and his Court*, pp.382–99.

46. See p.29. For further discussion of Llywarch, see pp.90, 119.

47. See pp.34, 81, 110, 112.

48. *Map*, pp.187–9.

49. *Journey*, p.88.

50. See L.B. Smith, 'The Gravamina of the community of Gwynedd against Llywelyn ap Gruffudd', *BBCS*, 31 (1984), 158–76; J.B. Smith, *Llywelyn*.

51. For the importance of such plunder to a king, see pp.27–8.

52. For more on this, see pp.94–5.

53. See Holm, 'Slave trade', 317–45; D. Ó'Cróinín, *Early Medieval Ireland, 400–1200* (Harlow, 1995), p.268; W. Davies, *Wales*, p.64; E.I. Bromberg, 'Wales and the mediaeval slave trade', *Speculum*, 17 (1942), 263–69.

54. See Barlow, *Edward*, p.140.

55. For a study of the varied economy of twelfth-century Deheubarth, see H. Pryce, 'In search of a medieval society: Deheubarth in the writings of Gerald of Wales', *WHR*, 13 (1986–87), 265–81.

56. *Journey*, p.196.

57. *Brut* (RBH), pp.26–7; *Brut* (Pen. 20), p.15; *Bren.*, pp.72–3.

58. *Vita Ædwardi Regis*, p.58.

59. *Triads*, pp.25, 27.

60. See Stenton, *Anglo-Saxon*, pp.369–70.

61. See Dark, *Civitas*, p.223.

62. *Map*, p.193.

63. For more on this incident, see pp.106–8.

64. *Vita Ædwardi Regis*, p.58.

65. See p.110.

66. *Bren.*, pp.72–3.

67. For discussion, see P. Mac Cana, *Celtic Mythology* (London, 1970), pp.64, 78.

68. *Gruffudd ap Cynan*, p.60.

69. For further discussion of the handing on of Gruffudd ap Llywelyn's trappings in this incident, see R.C. Stacey, 'Clothes talk from medieval Wales', in *The Welsh King and his Court*, pp.338–9, 343; D. J. Moore, *Gruffudd ap Cynan: A Collective Biography*, ed. K.L. Maund (Woodbridge, 1996), pp.7–8.

70. *Map*, pp.193–5.

71. Stacey, 'Clothes talk', p.338.

72. For more on this, see pp.117–20.

73. This was something denied to the Welsh prince Gruffudd ap Rhys in the twelfth century. He ravaged Llanbadarn Fawr in 1116, but never established his dominion in the area and consequently failed to act as a patron of the church. The Welsh chronicle tends to be harsh and dismissive of Gruffudd ap Rhys' rule and abilities.

74. *Brut* (Pen. 20), s.a. 1022.

75. *Brut* (RBH), s.a. 1039. See also *Brut* (Pen. 20), s.a. 1039; *Bren.*, s.a. 1039; *AC*, pp.23–4.

76. *Brut* (RBH), s.a. 1063.

77. *Brut* (RBH), s.a. 1116.

78. *Liber Landavensis. The Text of the Book of Llan Dav*, ed. J.G Evans and J. Rhys (Oxford, 1893), p.266; *LL*, pp.535–6.

79. See Brooke, *The Church and the Welsh Border*, pp.14, 93.

80. *LL*, pp.539–41.

81. See C. Brooke, 'St Peter of Gloucester and St Cadoc of Llancarfan', in N.K. Chadwick et al., *Celt and Saxon: Studies in the Early British Border* (Cambridge, 1963), pp.258–322.

82. W. Davies, 'Adding Insult to Injury: Power, Property and Immunities in Early Medieval Wales', in W. Davies and P. Fouracre (eds), *Property and Power in the Early Middle Ages* (Cambridge, 1995) pp.137–64. The incidents of particular relevance deal with the supposed activities in the south of two sixth-century kings of Gwynedd, Maelgwn Gwynedd and his son Rhun, the former described as 'reigning over all Britain'; see *Vitae*, pp.73–5, 137–9. King Rhain of Brycheiniog is another to confirm the freedoms of Cadog's church after the saint's help in a conflict between Brycheiniog and rulers from the south-east; *ibid.*, pp.79–81.

83. Gwynllyw was said to be a king whose seat of power was on Stow Hill in modern-day Newport, above the mouth of the Usk. He united his realm with Brycheiniog by marrying Gwladus, the daughter of the king of that region. Cadog was the son of Gwynllyw and Gwladus. Talgarth is named as one of the main courts in Brycheiniog, a status that it probably maintained in the eleventh century when Gruffudd was active nearby in Llangors and Glasbury-on-Wye.

84. J.E. Caerwyn Williams, *The Poets of the Welsh Princes*, revised edn (Cardiff, 1994), p.8; see also P. Mac Cana, *The Mabinogi* (Cardiff, 1992), p.22.

85. S. Davies, *The Mabinogion* (Oxford, 2007), p.xxvii.

86. See pp.32–3.

87. For comparison, amongst Welsh rulers of the early twelfth century, Gruffudd ap Cynan had two wives, while Cadwgan ap Bleddyn is said to have had five. In eleventh-century England, King Cnut first married Ælfgifu of Northampton before later marrying Emma of Normandy. The latter was

acknowledged everywhere as Cnut's lawful wife, but Ælfgifu was never put aside, acting like a queen in the north of England and even being appointed as regent of Norway on behalf of the son that she had borne the king. See Stenton, *Anglo-Saxon*, pp.397–8.

88. See Maund, *Ireland*, pp.67–8.

89. *Map*, p.187.

90. OV, II, p.138; J. Marx (ed.), *Guillaume De Jumieges: Gesta Normannorum Ducem* (Rouen & Paris, 1914), p.192.

91. Rees Davies noted that: 'The problem of partibility was exacerbated by the polygamous habits of many Welsh princes and by an inclusive law of legitimacy'; *Age*, p.71.

92. See Maund, 'Welsh alliances', p.187, n.39; S. Baxter, *The Earls of Mercia: Lordship and Power in Late Anglo-Saxon England* (Oxford, 2007), p.254.

93. *LL*, p.536, 539–41.

94. The Welsh-language versions of the chronicle name the sons of Gruffudd as Maredudd and 'Ithel', but the earlier Latin text of *Annales Cambriae* has Maredudd and Idwal. For more on this battle, see p.130.

95. This is the implication from later charters of her and her husband Osbern's descendants, but details of Nest's antecedents are sketchy and it is possible that the family would have been keen to choose a connection to the aristocracy of Mercia in the female line rather than to an obscure Welsh woman.

96. None of Gruffudd's sons are known to have had children of their own. It has been suggested that the Hywel ab Ithel who held Rhos and Rhufoniog before he was killed in 1118 may have been a grandson of Gruffudd's: see Maund, *Ireland*, p.113. Accepting this would mean that Gruffudd's son was named Ithel and not Idwal, disregarding the 1069 evidence of *Annales Cambriae*. Hywel ab Ithel is believed to have enjoyed power with the assistance of the sons of Bleddyn ap Cynfyn, and this seems unlikely if he was the son of the 'Ithel'/Idwal who was killed by Bleddyn in 1069. Gruffudd's progeny did survive through his daughter, Nest. She had a number of children from her marriage to Osbern fitz Richard.

5

THE KILLING
OF A KING

I F THE DEATH of Gruffudd's son had opened the way for political
intrigue within his realm, it was the demise of his closest ally – and
of that man's intended heir – that would herald disaster. Ælfgar of
Mercia had lost his eldest son, Burgheard, in early 1061 when he died on
a return journey from Rome.[1] Although he was young at the time of his
death, Burgheard was already part of an exclusive club of English secular
landholders with estate holdings worth in excess of £40. That he was set to
be his father's successor is further suggested by the fact that he had been in
Rome on a successful diplomatic mission to defend his family's ecclesiastical interests against the growing power of the Godwines. Ælfgar himself
passed away sometime between September and December 1062, leaving
his young and inexperienced son Edwin as the new Earl of Mercia.[2] This
event triggered a response from Harold that both guaranteed that the earl
would succeed to the throne of England, and drew the political map that
would lead to his downfall and death at Hastings in 1066. Had Ælfgar lived
it seems certain that the great earl, backed by his powerful alliance with
Gruffudd, would have blocked Harold's path to the throne.[3] The deaths of
both Ælfgar and Burgheard opened a window of opportunity for Harold to
break the Welsh-Mercian alliance, avenge his previous humiliations in his
dealings with Gruffudd, and win the glory that would further bolster his
claims to succeed Edward on the throne of England.

The Strike at Rhuddlan

In 1066 Harold would show his inclination for swift, arguably rash, military action, with rapid marches leading him to glory at the Battle of Stamford Bridge then disaster at Hastings. In the judgement of Frank Barlow, the biographer of the Godwines, Harold was 'always an opportunist'.[4] In 1062, the earl struck into Wales from Edward's Christmas court at Gloucester, leading a surprise campaign against Gruffudd in his palace at Rhuddlan as described in the *Anglo-Saxon Chronicle*: 'After Christmas Earl Harold went from Gloucester to Rhuddlan, which belonged to Gruffudd, and there he burnt the residence and the ships and all the equipment which belonged to them; and he put him to flight.'[5] John of Worcester supplies a fuller account:

> After Christmas, at the command of King Edward, Harold, the vigorous earl of the West Saxons, took a small troop of horsemen from Gloucester, where the king was then staying, and set out for Rhuddlan in great haste to kill Gruffudd, king of the Welsh, because of the frequent and destructive raids which he often made within the English borders and the disgrace which he often brought upon his lord King Edward. But Gruffudd, having learned in advance of his approach, took flight with his men, embarked on a ship, and just managed to escape. On learning of his flight, Harold ordered his palace to be burnt and his ships set on fire with their tackle, and turned back the same day.[6]

The account is at pains to stress that the attack was ordered by Edward and that it was in retaliation for Gruffudd's border raids. This theme is also highlighted in the *Life of King Edward*, which refers to the Welsh leader being 'discontented with his western bounds', 'carrying wrongful war across the Severn' and 'forcing England to endure his hostile blow'.[7] However, the border had been quiet since 1058, and part of the reason for Gruffudd having been caught off guard could have been that he felt secure with the peace treaty that he had agreed with Edward. The attitude of Edwin cannot be determined with certainty, and it is possible that the inexperienced youngster supported Harold's move. But it seems more likely that the new Mercian earl, who would have been grieving for his father, was himself caught off guard and knew nothing of Harold's plans. The accounts of Harold's subsequent campaigns against Gruffudd make no mention of the presence of Mercian troops, and in later years Edwin would renew his father's policy of alliance with Welsh leaders. The destruction of the Welsh king would seriously weaken Edwin's family's strategic position within England and allow Harold's dominance, and it is unlikely that the new earl was unaware of the dangers. Osbern fitz Richard is another member of the English nobility who may have had reason to oppose the attack on Rhuddlan. He was the son of Richard fitz Scrob, the founder of Richard's Castle and a man likely to have been among the leaders of the force defeated by Gruffudd in 1052. The families would be reconciled though, as Osbern had either already married Gruffudd's daughter, Nest, or was soon to. The accounts of Harold's motivation in John of Worcester and the *Life of King Edward* reflect the propaganda of the winning side and are able to present an easily understandable story of England v. Wales, ignoring the more complex background politics and the true nature of Harold's power grab.

Given all that is known of Gruffudd's career and his military skill, it seems remarkable that he was caught so badly off guard at Rhuddlan, but there are a number of possible explanations. The years of peace after 1058 may have played a part in dulling his senses as the ageing king enjoyed the riches of his hard-won realm. A clue to the failure of Gruffudd's intelligence system could also be found in the Welsh lawbooks. They make provision for the king's military household (W. *teulu*) to leave him after Christmas to enjoy a circuit of their lord's townships under the warband's leader, known as the *penteulu*. The *penteulu* and the household would then return to the king's side and would not leave him for the rest of the year.[8] Harold's winter strike was a surprise move, well away from the usual spring and summer campaign season, and it is possible that the earl had deliberately chosen the moment when he knew Gruffudd's warband was absent. Such timing signals Harold's skill as a military leader, while the intimate knowledge of Gruffudd's court could also suggest the presence of third-party informants, either from the Welsh king's allies in Mercia, or from within his own following. It should be noted that the slaying of Rhys ap Rhydderch was arranged under similar circumstances, the order being given at King Edward's Christmas court in Gloucester in 1052, and the

Welshman's head being delivered to the king on 5 January 1053. Perhaps the best explanation for the success of Harold's strike however, is the possibility that Ælfgar died at Edward's 1062 Christmas court. This would account for the speed of Harold's campaign, and would have left Gruffudd unaware of the passing of his ally and the danger that he was in, with even his friends in Mercia not knowing of their leader's demise.

The Final Campaign

Despite the disastrous failure of his intelligence, it seems that Gruffudd did receive a last-minute warning. This allowed him and his closest followers to board one of the ships at bay below the court on the River Clwyd and thereby make their escape. Harold's surgical strike had come close to complete success, but Gruffudd was now loose and alert to the danger from across the border. It is possible that his first move was to Ireland, where he may have sailed in search of allies, but our only sources for this, the late thirteenth- or early fourteenth-century chronicle of Pierre de Langtoft and the late eleventh-century German chronicler Adam of Bremen, are tenuous.[9] Such a move seems plausible; it was a venture that could have been suggested by Hiberno-Scandinavian crew on his ship or in his household, men who may have stayed with Gruffudd after the successful campaigns of 1055 and 1058. It should also be noted though, that Gruffudd's dynastic rival Cynan ab Iago was established in exile in Dublin, while the king of that city, Diarmait mac Máel na mBó, was an ally of Harold who had helped the earl in the crisis of 1052 and would harbour Harold's sons after his death at Hastings in 1066.[10] Langtoft says that Gruffudd returned to Wales after his trip to Ireland, and the king is next found in the heart of his kingdom preparing for Harold's onslaught. The earl had returned to England from Rhuddlan, perhaps to Edward's court at Gloucester, or to Oxford, as is suggested by the early twelfth-century Anglo-Norman chronicler Geoffrey Gaimar. Harold was soon engaged in planning a major new Welsh campaign for the spring of 1063, gathering an army and fleet that he would lead into south Wales while his brother, Tostig, led a land force into north Wales from his earldom of Northumbria.

We can be certain that Gruffudd's preparations for war were vigorous, but it was immediately apparent that the 'greater Wales' he had built with its expanded borders to the east was now unsustainable. These lands lacked natural defences, and without Mercia to act as a buffer territory they lay open to the full weight of Harold and Tostig's attack. Edwin is not recorded actively fighting against Gruffudd, but the propaganda in the surviving Anglo-Saxon sources that describe the war as being in revenge for the Welsh leader's border raids and humiliations of King Edward suggest that the new Mercian earl would have found it difficult to do much to help his father's ally. Gruffudd was forced to fall back to the wilder depths of Wales, and as he did so Harold was given the opportunity to gnaw away at the network of alliances that supported his rival, giving the fiercely independent localities of Wales the chance to restore their native dynasties. Even so, a general as effective as Gruffudd would be expected to mount a formidable defence of the rugged, inaccessible heartland of his kingdom. Unfortunately for the Welsh king, his enemy Harold was another man of uncommon military ability, drive and ambition.

Of the accounts of the campaign that rely upon contemporary sources, John of Worcester has the fullest version. His work agrees with the facts laid out in the *Anglo-Saxon Chronicle* but furnishes additional detail: 'About Rogationtide [25–28 May] [Harold] set out from Bristol with a naval force, and sailed around a great part of Wales. His brother Earl Tostig met him with mounted troops, as the king commanded, and they at once joined forces, and began to lay waste that region. By that the Welsh were coerced, and gave hostages.'[11] The decision to attack with a fleet from Bristol is intriguing given Gruffudd's suggested association with Portskewett on the opposite side of the Severn, and with other key centres with links to the sea such as Caerleon, Carmarthen, Carew, Aberystwyth, Caernarfon, Aberffraw, Aberlleiniog, Bangor, Abergwyngregyn, Degannwy and Rhuddlan. As Gruffudd used such sites to impose his dominion on Wales, Harold rolled back his rival's achievements by landing along the coast. An account of Harold's raiding in south-east Wales is contained in the *Life of St Gwynllyw*. The dating of the passage is unclear, with a sentence claiming that the attack on the saint's church on Stow Hill (modern-day St Woolo's, Newport) occurred a few months before the Battle of Hastings (14 October 1066).

But the overall context of the piece is set in the time when Gruffudd ap Llywelyn (described as the 'valiant king of all Wales' or '*regis fortis tocius Wallie*') was ruling in south-east Wales and when Edward was King of England, placing it in the period 1055–63. Harold's attack was said to be motivated by a disagreement over tolls levied by Gruffudd's officials against English traders on the River Usk, and it is likely that this was a pretext used by the earl for his intrusion into the area in 1063:

> Merchants frequently came from England, and exchanged wares at the mouth (or harbour) of the River Usk. After finishing they paid toll, and if they had not paid the usual custom, they would no more have had leave to land and to traffic up the river mouth. But it happened on one occasion that they were unwilling to pay. When this was heard, Rhiryd son of Ifor, nephew of King Gruffudd, proceeded to the river mouth (or shore) with anger, and full of indignation, ordered the debt to be paid, but for all such commandment they did not pay. Afterwards in derision and to the disgrace of the Englishmen he cut the rope of their anchor, and caused the freed anchor to be taken away to the church of St Gwynllyw. The sailors and the merchants having returned to the earl Harold, narrated the disgrace and the derision inflicted on them. Therefore the earl, ill-disposed, moved with very great anger and wishing to take vengeance, assembled an army. This being assembled, he invaded Glamorgan, hostilely determined to burn and to lay waste the whole region. This movement being heard of, the natives took their goods to the sanctuaries of the saints. When these were so taken, they fled and hid themselves in the woods. After the army had come, it burnt and ravaged, sparing none, seizing everything it found. In the meantime, the bar having been broken, some of the ravagers entered the church of the venerable Gwynllyw, which was full of garments and provisions and many precious things. When these were seen, like wolves most greedy for rapine, they seized everything which they had seen within the church. But the aforesaid anchor, which was the cause of the devastation and rapine, was seen by none, and yet it was in an inner corner of the church. Cheeses were divided by the robbers, but, when they were being cut into, they appeared bloody within; the whole army was astounded, restoring everything which it had seized, with ready hands. Moreover, the earl Harold among the first offered of his own

to the altar, being pricked with terrible compunction. Thence he returned, greatly fearing that more revenge would be taken, promising never to violate the sanctuary of the venerable church. Forthwith in the next month for that iniquity and for other transgressions he was conquered in the Battle of Hastings by King William and slain.[12]

The *Life of St Gwynllyw*, first composed late in the second half of the eleventh century, needs to be handled with great care as it seeks to outline and defend the supposed rights of the church that sponsored its composition. But there is no reason to doubt that it preserves a genuine memory of Harold's raiding in the area, and it is known that the earl was active there in 1063 and 1065. If the miraculous elements of the story can be discarded, it is possible that Harold's returning of plunder represented his appeasement of the church after his victory in 1063.

Gruffudd Deserted

Given the struggles that Gruffudd had faced in establishing his authority over areas such as south-east Wales, Ystrad Tywi and Dyfed, it is likely that many of the regions welcomed the opportunity offered by Harold's invasion to shed their allegiance to the northern king and restore their native nobility. Certainly, Gaimar claims that it was rebellion in south Wales that caused Gruffudd's downfall. Caradog, the son of Gruffudd ap Rhydderch who Gruffudd ap Llywelyn had killed in 1055, was soon ruling as the dominant king in the south-east from his base in upper Gwent, and Harold is unlikely to have found it difficult to persuade such a man to fight on his side. Caradog's attack on Harold's newly built hunting lodge at Portskewett in 1065 may have been a result of frustration that he had not received all that he felt he had been promised for his help in 1063, or a reaction to Harold pushing his territorial claims as Earl of Hereford into the lands on his western border. The poet Berddig's post-1063 power in Gwent and the description of Ednywain of Gwynedd as a 'most intimate friend' of Caradog could suggest that even Gruffudd ap Llywelyn's own men in the southeast did not prove reliable.[13] The Tudor historian David Powel claimed that Harold entered south Wales in 1063 'by the procurement of Caradoc ap Gruffyth ap Rytherch, and others'.[14] Caradog's cousin, Rhydderch ap Caradog, was surely a part of this alliance. He would come to hold dominion in lower Gwent and Ewias with a royal centre at Caerleon, in the area where Gruffudd ap Llywelyn's officer Rhiryd ab Ifor was active before the clash with Harold. The allegiances of the traditional rulers of Glamorgan are more difficult to determine. Their likely adherence to Gruffudd ap Llywelyn in 1055 has been noted, and the church at Llandaff profited under the northern king's rule. The church on Stow Hill that was attacked by Harold also has connections with the clerical family that dominated Llandaff and Llancarfan, and the *Life of St Gwynllyw* was a product of their scriptorium. But Meurig ap Hywel's son Cadwgan, who would hold dominion in Glamorgan after 1063, was a man from another ancient and proud royal line. He may have had ambitions of his own, or he may have swayed to Harold's side when the success of the English invasion was obvious.

Harold's undermining of Gruffudd's authority in the south-east was repeated in south-west Wales. Maredudd ab Owain was soon ruling there with the help of his brothers Hywel and Rhys, all nephews of Gruffudd's old rival for the rule of Deheubarth, Hywel ab Edwin. Harold's successes in the south were matched by Tostig's as he advanced along the north Wales coast with his force from Northumbria, and John Edward Lloyd suggested that the forces may have joined up on Anglesey.[15] Accounts in the *Anglo-Saxon Chronicle* and by John of Worcester seem to suggest that there was little resistance to the brother earls. But submissiveness is not what we would expect from Gruffudd, and his vigorous defence is suggested by the *Life of King Edward*. This account is somewhat poetic and muddled, describing the attack on Rhuddlan as the climax of the war rather than its beginning. It also has an editorial agenda in lauding the achievements of the house of Godwine when members of the family were prepared to work together. The text does, though, give a flavour of the guerrilla campaign that was waged by Gruffudd:

> [The 'Western Britons' are] a race bred in Caucasian rocks, untamed,
> And very strong when Gruffudd was their king,
> And discontented with the western bounds?

He carried wrongful war across the Severn,
And England's realm endured his hostile blow,
Until King Edward, marked by worth and fame,
Compelled him to regret the crime. For when
The English hastening under Harold joined
Fast columns and platoons of Tostig's men
They terrified the foe, till then so bold,
With close attack in strength, with fire and sword.
And though with many virtues he displayed
Th'ancestral glory of his chivalry,
Gruffudd, unequal to this fight, did fear
T'engage with these, and sought remote retreats.
Inured to lurk in distant dikes, from which
He can with safety fly upon the foe,
Exploiting barren lands with woods and rocks,
He galls the brother earls with drawn-out war.
And these, resourceful in a doubtful case,
Throw down the country in one general ruin.
The enemy's house is sacked, the girded chests
Are broached, and royal pomp exposed to loot.
In blaze of glory, ably led, the men
Return, and bring back this fine ornament:
They smashed a fleet – for Welsh control and lore
Was not the equal of the Ocean's chiefs –
And take a prow and stern of solid gold,
Cast by the smith's assiduous skill, and this,
With looted treasures and the hostages,
As proof of victory they give their king.[16]

The war had entered a phase common to combat in the Middle Ages: a clash characterised by ravaging, evasion and ambush. Pitched battles were avoided as opposing forces shadowed one another, seeking out their opponents' weaknesses, harrying their supplies and waiting for the moment of opportunity. Gruffudd is described as 'fearing to engage and seeking remote retreats', but he was following accepted tactical principles. That his tactics enjoyed a degree of success is suggested by the description of the Welsh 'flying with safety upon the foe' as Gruffudd 'galled the brother earls with drawn-out war'. The Welsh chronicle says that Gruffudd was located in 'the waste valleys', suggesting that he had retreated behind the most formidable natural defences in Wales, to Gwynedd Uwch Conwy, the mountainous heartland of Snowdonia to the west of the River Conwy. Only on the rarest occasions did an English invading force succeed in penetrating into this natural citadel. After the processional nature of Harold's early successes, the campaign had got bloody and dirty. The fact that both the earl and his brother, Tostig, were equal to the formidable military challenges they were facing was highlighted by the traditions preserved by two twelfth-century writers, John of Salisbury and Gerald of Wales. The context of the former's account was the failure of the English troops of his day (mid-twelfth century) to deal with the Welsh militarily as they placed too much reliance on heavy armour, leaving them unable to cope with the swift attacks made by their lightly clad enemies from their wild retreats. John contrasted this with the tactics employed in 1063:

> When [Harold] perceived the mobility of the foreigners, he selected for the mission soldiers who fought in the same way, since he resolved that they were to engage in battle practise in light armament, assaulting in rawhide boots, chests covered by hardened straps and hides, throwing up small light shields against the missiles, and at one time hurling javelins, at another employing swords against the enemy. His troops would stick close to the enemy's fleeing footsteps in order that they might hold fast 'foot to foot and spear to spear' and might repulse shield with shield. And so he devastated everything along the way to Snowdon and ... he captured their kings and presented their heads to the king who had sent him. And killing every male he could find, all the way to pitiful little children, he pacified the province with the edge of a sword.[17]

Gerald of Wales entitles a chapter in his book *The Description of Wales* 'The sins of the Welsh, through which they lost first Troy and then Britain'. The section follows on from his advice on how to overcome the Welsh, a passage that it has been suggested was used as the model for Edward I's eventual wars of conquest in 1277–83. Gerald's instructions seem to be modelled on Harold's campaign of 1063 as he advises a joint land and naval campaign, the use of lightly armed troops to penetrate the country and combat Welsh ravagers, the blockading of the country by land and sea, and the sowing of dissension among Welsh ranks 'using promises and bribes to stir them up against each other'. Gerald outlines the efforts made by the Anglo-Saxon kings to reduce the Welsh, highlighting Æthelfrith's victory in battle at Chester *c.* 616[18] and Offa 'shutting the Welsh off' with his dyke in the eighth century:

> Then, last of all, and by far the greatest, came Harold. He advanced into Wales on foot, at the head of his lightly clad infantry, lived on the country, and marched up and down and round and about the whole of Wales with such energy that he 'left not one that pisseth against a wall'. In commemoration of his success, and to his own undying memory, you will find a great number of inscribed stones put up in Wales to mark the many places where he won a victory. This was the old custom. The stones bear the inscription: HIC FUIT VICTOR HAROLDUS. It is to these recent victories of the English over the Welsh, in which so much blood was spilt, that the first three kings of the Normans owe the fact that in their lifetime they have held Wales in peace and subjection.[19]

In the face of such co-ordinated aggression, and with his own support being whittled away, Gruffudd's resistance to the onslaught lasted a little over two months. If the lack of loyalty shown by his clients in the south-east and south-west was perhaps predictable, a more mortal blow was struck when Gruffudd's half-brothers Bleddyn and Rhiwallon went over to Harold. Their powerbase and sphere of influence is thought to have been in Powys, where they are likely to have served as key lieutenants of Gruffudd. Perhaps the rigours of the campaign had worn them out, or perhaps the death of Owain ap Gruffudd in 1059 had made them realise that they could succeed Gruffudd and rule in Wales. The later alliance of Bleddyn's successor, Trahaearn, with Caradog ap Gruffudd could also suggest that Bleddyn himself had made some sort of compact with Caradog.[20] Pierre de Langtoft has this account:

> Gruffudd has two brothers, the king
> Wishes to conciliate them.
> Bleddyn and Rhiwallon, so I heard them named,
> They were accustomed to support the king's part
> In all the wars which Gruffudd raised;
> Therefore the king caused them to be
> Enfeoffed in his lands,
> And he took their homages of them.[21]

John of Worcester says that the Welsh: 'surrendered, and promised that they would pay him tribute, and they deposed and outlawed their king Gruffudd.'[22] This suggests that Gruffudd fought on with a handful of his closest companions, probably his military household (W. *teulu*), even after his key allies had gone over to Harold and repudiated his authority. Gruffudd was probably holding out in the wilds of Snowdonia or Meirionnydd, but Harold would not let his prey off the hook. The *Anglo-Saxon Chronicle* records the date and manner of Gruffudd's eventual demise:

> In autumn King Gruffudd was killed on 5 August by his own men because of the fight he fought against Earl Harold. He was king over all the Welsh, and his head was brought to Earl Harold, and Harold brought it to the king, and the figurehead of his ship and the ornaments with it. And King Edward entrusted the country to the two brothers of Gruffudd, Bleddyn and Rhiwallon, and they swore oaths and gave hostages to the king and the earl, promising that they would be faithful to him in everything, and be everywhere ready on water and on land, and likewise would pay such dues from that country as had been given before to any other king.[23]

The Welsh chronicle has no information on the campaign that led to Gruffudd's downfall, neglecting to even mention English involvement but instead concentrating on the 'treacherous' aspect of his death:

> Gruffudd ap Llywelyn was slain, after innumerable victories and taking of spoils and treasures of gold and silver and precious purple raiment, through the treachery of his own men, after his fame and glory had increased and after

he has aforetimes been unconquered, but was now left in the waste valleys, and after he had been head and shield and defender to the Britons.[24]

An Intimate Assassination

It is not difficult to draw up a list of suspects in trying to identify Gruffudd's killer. Caradog ap Gruffudd, Rhydderch ap Caradog, Cadwgan ap Meurig, and the sons of Owain – Maredudd, Hywel and Rhys – would each stand to enjoy power in south Wales after Gruffudd's demise. All (with the possible exception of Cadwgan) had both the personal and political motivations for wanting the king dead, and would have been unlikely to hesitate if his neck was at their mercy. But such men would not have been in Gruffudd's trusted inner circle and would not, therefore, have been among the die-hard followers who were with him at the end. Bleddyn and Rhiwallon may have been among their half-brother's most trusted supporters, and the positions of authority they secured from Harold after Gruffudd's demise gives them the motivation to have betrayed him. John of Worcester's account suggests that Gruffudd fought on after his brothers' defection, however, again leaving them out of the small group that was with the king at the end.

It is possible that Gruffudd was killed by members of his household (W. *teulu*) who lacked a political motivation but had simply had enough of their protracted war as they 'lurked in distant dykes' in an increasingly hopeless cause. But such a slaying would break all the accepted rules of society that governed the duties owed by a *teulu* to its lord. The *Gododdin*, arguably the greatest Welsh poem of the early Middle Ages and a work that would have been sung in courts throughout the country, gloried in the loyalty of the household of Mynyddog Mwynfawr, who followed their lord on a suicide mission that meant certain death to all. Households that abandoned their lord when his need was greatest earned everlasting infamy in Welsh literature and were described in the *Triads* – something of an instruction book for would-be bards – as the 'Three Faithless Warbands of Britain'. One of the households, that of Goronwy the Radiant of Penllyn, is described in the prose tale *Math*. Goronwy is the villain of the piece, a treacherous cuckolder who had planned to murder the hero Lleu, but his *teulu* are castigated in the strongest terms for failing to volunteer for certain death in place of their dishonoured lord when his crime is uncovered.

The notices of Gruffudd's death in Welsh, English and continental sources have been considered, but the historical traditions of another country have claims to a more definitive identification of the king's killer. Two related Irish chronicles – *The Annals of Ulster* and *The Annals of Loch Cé* – say that Gruffudd was slain by a 'son of Iago', undoubtedly a reference to the offspring of Iago ab Idwal, who Gruffudd had replaced as King of Gwynedd in 1039. It has been noted that Cynan ab Iago had found refuge in exile in Dublin under Harold's ally, Diarmait mac Máel na mBó, and that Cynan may have been involved in attacks on Gruffudd in 1042 and 1052. Moreover, Benjamin Hudson has pointed out that another less well-known Irish source, found in British Library MS Add. 30512, actually names Cynan ab Iago as Gruffudd's killer.[25] The outlawing and rejection of Gruffudd by his own people may have encouraged Cynan to return to Wales and attempt to claim the kingship of Gwynedd. The *History of Gruffydd ap Cynan* uniquely states that Cynan was a king of Gwynedd and, while this title was not generally recognised, it is possible that he was able to secure some sort of spurious claim to the position in the confused summer of 1063. Diarmait would have motivation to back such an adventure, perhaps with the connivance of his ally Harold. In succeeding years Hiberno-Scandinavian mercenaries would provide the major backing for Cynan's son, Gruffudd, as he made a series of attempts to establish himself in Gwynedd, and it may be speculated that he was following his father's example. David Wyatt notes that the Hiberno-Scandinavians were making increasing claims to overlordship for parts of Britain at this time, and that they had a particular interest in Anglesey.[26] Fresh slave trading opportunities were a major part of their motivation, with the native Irish reconquest of Dublin in 1052 limiting chances at home, while the increasingly powerful Anglo-Saxon state was proving a formidable foe. Wales, too, had become a much tougher target under Gruffudd ap Llywelyn, and the chance to fragment his kingdom would have been welcome.

It is probable that Gruffudd ap Llywelyn's final redoubt was in the wilds of Snowdonia. In the narrow dynastic world of Welsh politics, it is likely that among Gruffudd's remaining followers were men connected to Cynan ab Iago, either through blood or through service to his father. It has already been noted that a relative of Cynan's, Tangwystl, was the wife of Gruffudd's 'most trusted treasurer and chamberlain' Llywarch Olbwch, and that she had been close enough to the king after his death to have secured 'the thinnest and finest shirt and tunic made from the mantle of King Gruffudd'. The possible link between Gruffudd's treasurer and chamberlain and the Llywarch named by Walter Map as a nephew of the king has been noted. If the two names can be connected, it would seem that Gruffudd's initial wariness of the youthful Llywarch had been well founded. The chronicler Orderic Vitalis uniquely claims that Gruffudd was decapitated in his bath. The tale – contained in an interpolation into William of Jumièges' *Gesta Normannorum Ducum* – may have been invented as a stock literary conceit. But Orderic was born in Shropshire *c.* 1075 and maintained a strong interest in the Welsh border after he became a monk at Saint-Évroult; it is just possible that he has preserved a memory of the intimate nature of Gruffudd's assassination.

That Cynan ab Iago could, from a base on Anglesey or the mainland of Gwynedd, have contacted his connections within Gruffudd's inner circle and engineered the beleaguered king's demise seems a more than plausible conclusion. The fact that there is no mention of Cynan having played such a role in the *History of Gruffydd ap Cynan* has been seen as an argument against this, but the omission can be explained. The latter text was written to emphasise the legitimate right to rule of Cynan's son Gruffudd and his descendants. Gruffudd ap Cynan's heritage from kings is repeatedly stressed, including his link in the direct male line to Rhodri Mawr, a dynastic connection that Gruffudd ap Llywelyn did not claim, which would lead later historiography to view him as something of a 'usurper'. At the time of the writing of the *History of Gruffydd ap Cynan* however, the extraordinary achievements of Gruffudd ap Llywelyn would have been well remembered, as indicated by the transmission of the folk tales of Walter Map and by the notice of other twelfth-century writers. While omitting the details of Gruffudd ap Llywelyn's death, the *History of Gruffydd ap Cynan* is keen to associate its own hero with the trappings and glory of the former king through the receiving of his effects of state. Cynan, in contrast, was such an obscure figure that his son Gruffudd was often described as 'grandson of Iago' rather than 'son of Cynan'. Cynan was anonymous in Wales; a man who had spent most of his life in exile in Ireland and whose attempts to return to the land of his father relied upon Hiberno-Scandinavian military support. For such a man to have killed a great king like Gruffudd ap Llywelyn at a time when he was resisting a brutal English attack on Wales can hardly have been a claim to glory. Moreover, the manner of Gruffudd's death and the treatment of his remains did little credit to those responsible. Our sources suggest the treacherous and intimate nature of Gruffudd's betrayal, while the delivery of his head to an alien king who was not personally responsible for the killing has been called 'inappropriate and shameful'.[27] The descendants of Cynan through his son Gruffudd would, in the twelfth and thirteenth centuries, become the most famous princes of medieval Wales, and would include Owain Gwynedd, Llywelyn ab Iorwerth ('Llywelyn the Great') and Llywelyn ap Gruffudd ('Llywelyn the Last'). It was from the patronage and propaganda of these men that many of the historical traditions of Wales were formed, including the emphasis on the importance of the descendants of Rhodri Mawr to the detriment of other dynastic lines. Even so, the memories of the glories of Gruffudd ap Llywelyn could not be forgotten and were preserved in the records of the Welsh chronicle. The weight of circumstantial and external evidence would suggest that Cynan ab Iago played at least a part in the treacherous slaying of Gruffudd ap Llywelyn. That the Welsh historical tradition preserves no record of his role in this should not be a surprise.

Notes

1. See S. Baxter, 'The death of Burgheard son of Ælfgar and its context' in P. Fouracre and D. Ganz (eds), *Frankland. The Franks and the World of the Early Middle Ages. Essays in honour of Dame Jinty Nelson* (Manchester, 2008), pp.266–84.

2. Ælfgar was addressed in two of King Edward's charters dated 8 September 1062, but was dead by the time of Harold's raid on Rhuddlan.

3. This was the conclusion drawn by Frank Stenton; see his *Anglo-Saxon England*, pp.575–6.

4. Barlow, *Godwins*, p.130.

5. *ASC* (D), 1063.

6. JW, p.593.

7. See pp.112–13.

8. '[The *penteulu*] is entitled to a circuit from the king, after he parts from him at Christmas, together with the *teulu*', *Law*, p.11. One of the Llandaff charters, claiming to be from the period 1056–63, purports to tell the story of the *teulu* of Cadwgan ap Meurig of Glamorgan acting without the controlling influence of their king on Christmas Day. They are said to have visited the church at Llandaff where 'being elated with the excessive rejoicings of so great a festivity, they began to be riotous'. In their drunken state the warriors killed a clergyman, an event that resulted in a reparation grant to Llandaff, *LL*, pp.537–9.

9. 'Harold went towards Wales with very noble heart. When Harold came there, Gruffudd has passed the sea straight to Ireland, he dared not remain.' T. Wright (ed.), *The Chronicle of Pierre de Langtoft*, I, 2 vols (London, 1866–68) pp.392–5; *Adam of Bremen: The History of the Archbishops of Hamburg-Bremen*, trans. F.J. Tschan (New York, 1959), p.126.

10. See Maund, *Ireland*, pp.164–5; Barlow, *Edward*, p. 120.

11. JW, p.593.

12. *Vitae*, p.187.

13. See p.83.

14. Powel, *Historie*, p.101.

15. Lloyd, 'Wales and the coming', p.137.

16. *Vita Ædwardi Regis*, p.87.

17. John of Salisbury, *Policraticus*, ed. C.J. Nederman (Cambridge, 1990), p.114.

18. For more on this, see S. Davies, 'The Battle of Chester and warfare in post-Roman Britain', *History*, 95 (2010), 143–58.

19. *Description*, p.266. No examples of the inscribed stones described by Gerald have ever been found.

20. For this suggestion, see Maund, *Ireland*, pp.70, 74.

21. Langtoft, *Chronicle*, pp.393–6.

22. JW, p.593.

23. *ASC* (D), 1063.

24. *Brut* (Pen. 20), s.a. 1063.

25. B.T. Hudson, 'The destruction of Gruffudd ap Llywelyn', *WHR*, 15 (1990–91), 331–50.

26. See D. Wyatt, 'Gruffudd ap Cynan and the Hiberno-Norse World', *WHR*, 19 (1999), 595–617. Wyatt claims that Gruffudd ap Cynan was something of a 'Hiberno-Scandinavian pawn' but that, given his early obscurity in Wales, 'he may have been a willing one'.

27. F.C. Suppe, 'The cultural significance of decapitation in high medieval Wales and the Marches', *BBCS*, 36 (1989), 147–60.

6

GRUFFUDD'S LEGACY

ANY HISTORIANS HAVE been notably dismissive of the achievements of Gruffudd, Norman Davies summing up his reign thus: 'In a 30-year rampage of violence against all his neighbours, he murdered and marauded his way to a fitting end.'[1] Rees Davies was more generous in acknowledging the success of the king during his lifetime, but found the lack of a legacy from his reign somewhat troubling: 'Within Wales itself his [Gruffudd's] death left a vacuum of authority and power. His hegemony had been founded on military might and personal dependence; it had no institutional base which could outlast his own downfall.'[2] Such damning verdicts seem somewhat harsh on Gruffudd. His achievements at the height of his power were unequalled by any independent Welsh ruler, having secured control and recognition of a devolved state of greater Wales within the British Isles. The death of his eldest son may have damaged his plans for a secure succession, before the untimely demise of his closest ally Ælfgar opened up the defences of his realm. Even then he may have avoided disaster, were he not facing in Harold one of the most vigorous and effective of Anglo-Saxon leaders, and a man who had not the slightest compunction in breaking the peace treaty that Gruffudd had made with King Edward. It was the disloyalty of the Welsh king's own countrymen and kinsmen that sealed his fate, while the propaganda that would emanate from the families of these same people would play its part in diminishing the reputation of Gruffudd in the eyes of history. But, if the enemies of the great king ensured that he would not secure a lasting legacy, it can be seen that the effort needed to destroy Gruffudd had created fatal flaws in the power bases of all those responsible for his death.

Britain after Gruffudd: Conquest and Colonisation

Harold's surprise strike against Gruffudd at Rhuddlan after Christmas 1062 can be seen as the first link in a chain of events that would lead to his winning the throne of England, and also to the last Anglo-Saxon king's defeat and death at Hastings. Had Harold been facing the unbroken power bloc of Mercia and Wales when Edward the Confessor died at the beginning of 1066, it seems inconceivable that he would have been allowed to claim the Crown. The most likely successor would have been the last surviving male member of the ancient line of the kings of Wessex, Edgar Ætheling, the son of Edward's nephew. He was the logical compromise candidate, and would have been able to rule with the support and influence of his leading nobles, as Edward himself had done when he arrived from Normandy. Edgar was born and raised in Hungary but had been brought to England in 1057 at the age of 5, following a European-wide search for potential heirs by the childless Edward. The title of Ætheling was bestowed on the boy, suggesting the community of the realm's acceptance of his throne-worthy status, but in 1066 his youth and lack of political allies in England prevented him from making an effective claim to succeed Edward.[3] After Hastings, the remaining Anglo-Saxon earls and bishops recognised the Ætheling as king, but Frank Barlow says that it would have been 'suicidal' for Ælfgar's sons Edwin and Morcar to have offered such support in opposition to Harold.[4] The latter's victorious 1063 Welsh campaign had boosted his prestige and cemented his position as the pre-eminent nobleman in England. Mercia was the only significant part of the country left outside the direct control of Harold or his immediate family, and the destruction of Gruffudd had neutered Edwin's potential for independent action. Edwin and Morcar would continue to forge effective alliances with the Welsh, but the military might available from Gruffudd's successors was not comparable to the support that he had offered in 1055 and 1058, when Harold and Edward had been compelled to make peace with Ælfgar and his supporters.

Harold had achieved dominance in England while shattering the political harmony of the land. His support of Bleddyn and Rhiwallon in Wales could be seen as an attempt to further usurp the position of Ælfgar's family by taking their old Welsh alliance and attaching it directly to himself as overlord.

Gruffudd's successors needed English support to further their ambitions of overlordship within Wales.[5] Bleddyn and Rhiwallon would remain true to their Mercian alliance, but this was not necessarily in opposition to the will of Harold. There are suggestions that Harold used his position of power after 1063 to try to heal the rifts that he had widened in the realm. In 1065 Northumbria revolted against the unpopular rule of Tostig. Morcar was proclaimed as the new earl, his position bolstered by the support of Edwin and his Welsh allies, and Harold chose to take their side against his brother, forcing Tostig into exile in Flanders.[6] The latter's misfortunes may even have been instigated by his involvement in the 1063 war against Gruffudd. This was the first time in centuries that a Northumbrian leader had played such a central role in a Welsh campaign and it may not have been a decision that found favour with his leading nobles. The 1065 revolution was sparked by a large tax increase that Tostig levied on his thegns, and it has been suggested that this was necessary because the earl had emptied his coffers in 1063.[7]

Although Harold and his brother had been hugely effective at campaigning together on the Welsh campaign, the relations between the two were never close ones.[8] Tostig now joined a growing band of powerful men outside England who were eyeing the fractured country expectantly, awaiting the death of Edward and their chance to claim a share of his rich land. Chief among these were two men with designs on the throne itself: Harold Hardrada, King of Norway, and William the Bastard, Duke of Normandy. Edward died of natural causes on 5 January 1066. Earl Harold of Wessex became King Harold II of England after his coronation the following day, but the new monarch was desperately in need of dependable allies. Having supported Edwin and Morcar in 1065, he moved to secure their allegiance by marrying their sister, Ealdgyth, the widow of his old enemy Gruffudd, who therefore went from being Queen of Wales to Queen of England. There is no evidence to suggest that Edwin and Morcar resisted Harold's succession to the throne, but equally little to suggest that they did much to help him as king. Even if the brothers supported Harold, it is likely that many of the leading men within their earldoms were less than enthusiastic about their new monarch.[9] Northumbria did not immediately recognise the new ruler and Harold was forced to travel there soon after his coronation. Given the strong connections between the north of England and Scandinavia, it is certain that word of this feeling against the new king would have reached Hardrada. The Norwegian king, who had made alliance with Tostig, struck the first major blow against Harold, landing with a force of over 300 ships in the north of England in early September.

It would have been well remembered that Hardrada's son, Magnus, had mounted his own raid into England in 1058. Magnus fought alongside Gruffudd and Ælfgar and the trio made a common peace with King Edward and Harold, suggesting that independent action from the Norwegian contingent was not an option. In 1066, the defence of the north was in the hands of Ælfgar's sons, Edwin and Morcar. Although they had Welsh troops in their ranks, this was not the mighty host that had been commanded by Gruffudd. If such an established Mercian–Welsh alliance still existed in 1066 it would surely have deterred any threat to the north, but the balance of power had been upset by the events of 1063. Hardrada met up with Tostig on the Tyne before sailing down the Yorkshire coast, ravaging Cleveland, Scarborough and Holderness before harbouring at Riccall on the Ouse and marching on York. When Hardrada landed, Harold was in the south awaiting the expected invasion of William and his army from Normandy. On 20 September, Edwin and Morcar were heavily defeated by Hardrada at Fulford Gate, 2 miles south of York, the earls putting up a brave fight but suffering grievous losses. The fact that York then fell with barely a fight suggests the unpopularity of Harold's rule amongst the general population in the north, and meant that forces from the south would have to fight a war on two fronts. Hardrada and his troops took up temporary camp at Stamford Bridge, 7 miles east of York, as they made the arrangements that would allow them to march on southern England.

These events impelled Harold to make his famous forced march to York, reaching Tadcaster, 9 miles south of the city, on 24 September. Revealing the boldness and impetuosity that he had displayed at Rhuddlan in 1062–63, the king surprised Hardrada's force at Stamford Bridge the following day. The invaders had failed to plan an adequate defence of a bridge over the Derwent, and the speed of the English attack allowed the native forces to drive into the heart of the invading force. Hardrada and Tostig were killed in a bloody battle, the remains of their army fleeing to Riccall where they needed just twenty-four of their ships to take them back to

Norway. Harold had won his greatest victory, but before he had a chance to enjoy the glory and spoils, word reached him that William and his army had landed at Pevensey on the undefended south coast on 28 September. Harold's reaction was, again, almost instantaneous. Within thirteen days at most, he marched back to London, regrouped what he could of his forces, and marched the additional 50 miles to challenge William at the duke's base in Hastings. Frank Barlow considered that Harold's actions in 1066 were: 'marked by extreme self-confidence. He had achieved, perhaps, even more than he had expected. But, always an opportunist, he may have started to push his luck a little too hard.'[10] His haste meant that he could not gather all the forces at his disposal, and the sources suggest that he had harnessed less than half the strength of England. William's scouts sited their enemy on 13 October, and on the following day the duke led his army up Senlac Hill to kill Britain's last Anglo-Saxon king and win the most famous battle in the country's history.

In his October campaign Harold had no support from Edwin and Morcar, nor from any of the lands in the north of his realm. Edwin and Morcar had, of course, been weakened by Fulford Gate, and ensuring the security of the north would have been their primary concern. After Hastings, however, they were among the leaders of a large army with the Ætheling that sought to defend London as William made his slow, meticulous and brutal approach on the city. Archbishop Aldred of York, Edwin, Morcar and other leading men elected the Ætheling as king in London, but there was no coronation and as William's victory became inevitable, the party submitted to the Conqueror. The revolts of the following years would show that significant native military forces remained at large in Anglo-Saxon England, but that they lacked a universally acceptable leader. Harold's actions in the critical months of 1066 have the frenetic quality of a man who was not certain of his support base and who needed dramatic action and victory to forestall pretenders. The last Anglo-Saxon king was a man whose power play in 1062–63 had ensured his effective usurpation of the throne, but in reshaping the political balance of the country and displacing the legitimate royal line he had fatally weakened the realm.

Wales After Gruffudd: From Kingdom to Principality

The death of Gruffudd led to a decline in status for Wales and the Welsh in every aspect that we may choose to consider. This was immediately obvious in the agreements made with the English Crown by the Welsh nobles seeking to succeed to Gruffudd's position. His half-brothers were the men emplaced by the victorious English forces, as recorded by the *Anglo-Saxon Chronicle*: 'King Edward entrusted the country to the two brothers of Gruffudd, Bleddyn and Rhiwallon, and they swore oaths and gave hostages to the king and the earl [Harold], promising that they would be faithful to him in everything, and be everywhere ready on water and on land, and likewise would pay such dues from that country as had been given before to any other king.'[11] The contrast between this agreement and the peace deal forced from England by Gruffudd c. 1056 could not have been greater. In the 1050s, Gruffudd's military might and political skill had compelled the Anglo-Saxon state to make a treaty that acknowledged the Welsh king's position at the height of his powers. Although there is a suggestion that Gruffudd accepted a role as an under-king to Edward, this had no practical implications and he owed no dues to England, materially or militarily. The situation seems more akin to the relationship that would develop between the Scottish and English Crowns. In contrast, Bleddyn and Rhiwallon sought peace from a position of complete subjection to the Anglo-Saxon state, perhaps even needing English military support to secure their claim to kingship within Wales. They promised military service and the payment of dues to Edward, and, in a further humiliation, had to give hostages on top of their sworn oaths in order to seal the deal. The Book of Llandaff would later call the two kings 'servants' of William the Conqueror.

The most striking sign of Wales' diminished status was in terms of territory. Gruffudd's career had been characterised by the drive for a greater Wales as, from north to south, he pushed the country's borders eastwards, reclaiming 'British' land that had been in the hands of the conquering Anglo-Saxons for centuries.[12] But the 1086 Domesday Book survey and other evidence shows that his land gains were reversed after his death, with Offa's Dyke re-established as the border.[13] The twelfth-century writer John of Salisbury claims that, after his victory in 1063, Harold established a law whereby any Welshman found with a weapon beyond the Dyke would be deprived of their hand and 'thereby the strength of the Britons was so impaired by the Duke that almost the entire nation seemed to die out and their women were married to Englishmen by the indulgence of the king'.[14] Indeed, the scale of the Welsh defeat in 1063 invited further conquests from England. While Bleddyn and Rhiwallon had ambitions to establish some sort of overlordship in Wales from their powerbase in Gwynedd and Powys after 1063, the immediate ambition of southern nobles like Caradog ap Gruffudd and Maredudd ab Owain was simply to re-establish their dynasties in their traditional localities. But Caradog, who is likely to have been one of Harold's earliest native adherents in his Welsh campaigns, soon suffered the indignity of seeing the earl encroaching on his family's heartlands in south-east Wales. When Harold decided to build a lavish hunting lodge at the ancient Welsh royal centre of Portskewett in 1065, it was a step too far. Caradog attacked, razing the building to the ground and slaughtering the workmen, perhaps reflecting his rejection of the imposition of a new form of territorial overlordship. The dramatic events of 1066 meant that there was no response from Harold, but the legacy he left of Wales as a land open to conquests would be passed on to the ambitious Normans when they arrived on the border.

The Welsh nobles who succeeded Gruffudd were soon engaged in a bewildering series of civil wars, with battles and political murders commonplace. The arrival of the Normans exacerbated the problem; their military opportunism offering encouragement and succour to would-be Welsh kings while the newcomers relentlessly carved out chunks of the country for themselves. Raiders from across the Irish Sea were also back on the scene, no longer kept in check by the power of Gruffudd. The Welsh chronicle records attacks in 1073 and 1080, while the support they offered to Cynan ab Iago and his son Gruffudd, the future King of Gwynedd and perhaps a Hiberno-Scandinavian client, has been noted.

After Caradog's 1065 assault on Portskewett, the first known challenge to the political order that had been established by Harold in Wales came in 1069. This suggests that Bleddyn and Rhiwallon had been weakened by the fall of the Anglo-Saxons. Harold, who had recognised their succession in Wales, fell in 1066, before the brothers' Mercian allies had their power broken in the 1067–69 revolts against Norman rule. In 1069 Bleddyn and Rhiwallon faced Gruffudd ap Llywelyn's sons, Maredudd and Idwal, at the Battle of Mechain, located in the vicinity of the village of Llansantffraid-ym-Mechain, 8 miles south-west of Oswestry and close to the suggested royal centre at Plas-yn-Dinas. It does not seem that Maredudd and Idwal had inherited their father's military skill, as Idwal was killed in the battle, while Maredudd 'died of cold in flight' in its aftermath. In a bloody day for the family, Rhiwallon was also killed in the battle, leaving Bleddyn as the sole ruler of Powys and Gwynedd, with, it seems, a tenuous claim to over-lordship over south Wales, perhaps including the direct rule of Ceredigion and of Brycheiniog. Bleddyn was the founder of the second dynasty of Powys, which would re-establish the kingdom's separate identity from that of Gwynedd for the first time since the ninth century. Nevertheless, his authority was never comparable to that of Gruffudd ap Llywelyn, and Wales fragmented under his rule. Bleddyn would meet an unfortunate end in 1075, when he was enticed south to exert his rule in Ystrad Tywi and was 'treach-erously' killed by the man who had sent the invitation, Rhys ab Owain.

Having re-established themselves in 1063, the petty kings of the south were soon engaged in their own battles for supremacy in the area, with their clashes focusing on the claims of Caradog ap Gruffudd in the south-east and Maredudd ab Owain in the south-west. Caradog killed Maredudd on the banks of the River Rhymney in 1072 with the help of Norman mercenaries, but could not stop the succession of Maredudd's brother Rhys in Deheubarth. After Rhys engineered the death of Bleddyn in 1075, the latter was succeeded in Gwynedd and Powys by Trahaearn ap Caradog of Arwystli, who may have been a cousin of Bleddyn's. The bloodletting con-tinued, with Trahaearn and Caradog ap Gruffudd allying to destroy Rhys in 1078 before some sort of order was established at Mynydd Carn in 1081. The battle, located within a day's march of St David's, resulted in the sur-prise defeat and death of both Trahaearn and Caradog at the hands of the exile Gruffudd ap Cynan and Rhys ap Tewdwr of Deheubarth, Rhys ab Owain's second cousin and his successor as king. While the battle allowed Rhys ap Tewdwr to secure a measure of authority over south-east as well as south-west Wales, it also opened up Gwynedd and parts of south-east Wales to further Norman penetration and conquest.

If the intricacies of such political chaos were lost on outside observers of Wales, the overall impression was not, and it served to emphasise the change that had been wrought since the demise of Gruffudd. The passing of the former king had been well recorded in Irish sources, and even in Germany by Adam of Bremen, but it is the universal acknowledgement of Gruffudd's unique status from English sources that is most striking. The *Life of King Edward* said that the 'Western Britons' were 'very strong' when Gruffudd was their king, while in the stark words of the twelfth-century Anglo-Norman chronicler Geoffrey Gaimar, there was 'no heed paid to the Welsh' after the death of Gruffudd. Gerald of Wales gives a back-handed compliment to the power of the former king by outlining the scale of the impact of Harold's victory and by describing: 'Gruffudd ap Llywelyn, who for so long had oppressed all Wales by his tyranny.'[15] The pride that Bernard de Neufmarché, the Norman conqueror of Brycheiniog, took in his associa-tion with Gruffudd through his marriage to the Welshman's granddaughter, Nest, is also suggested by Gerald.[16] Gruffudd's impact is best revealed in the work of Walter Map, however, whose folk tales show the aura that had built up around the Welsh king's name in the century after his downfall. Map refers to the Welsh as his compatriots, indicating that he was of Welsh descent, and his knowledge of the Anglo-Norman March of Wales is obvi-ous. He would have been well aware of other famous Welsh leaders of his day, including Gruffudd ap Cynan, Owain Gwynedd, Madog ap Maredudd and Rhys ap Gruffudd ('the Lord Rhys'), yet Gruffudd ap Llywelyn was the only one he chose to deal with in any detail.

The tone taken by English and continental sources in dealing with Welsh nobles became increasingly patronising in the course of the twelfth and thirteenth centuries, a reflection of growing imperial outlooks and of a very real reduction in the power of Welsh leaders. The attitude stands in stark contrast to the neutral tone taken by Anglo-Saxon sources in their deal-ings with Wales and ties in with the growing idea that cultures on the edge of mainstream Europe were 'barbaric'.[17] David Crouch contends that the Norman invaders regarded Welsh kingship as 'piffling' in comparison to their idea of the power and status demanded by such a title.[18] John of Worcester's take on the death of Rhys ap Tewdwr in 1093 was that 'from that day kings ceased to rule in Wales'. Gerald of Wales reports an early twelfth-century conversation between Earl Milo of Hereford and Gruffudd ap Rhys, the son and heir of Rhys ap Tewdwr. They were returning from the court of King Henry I, passing Llangors in Milo's dominion of Brycheiniog, when the earl began 'chaffing Gruffudd about his claim to noble blood'.[19] The Welshman took the teasing in good humour and succeeded in turning the joke on his travelling companion. Any feeling of triumph, however, must have been sour for Gruffudd, who was travelling through the Welsh sub-kingdom that his father had lost to the Normans when he was killed in 1093 while trying to uphold his claim to be regarded as 'king of the Britons'. A description of a group of Henry II's knights on campaign in the second half of the twelfth century is even more revealing, proclaiming that 'nor is there one of them who does not think himself worth of a Welsh king'.[20] In preparing for the Third Crusade, Richard I 'accepted a pledge from the petty kings of the Welsh and Scots that whilst he was on pilgrimage they would not cross their borders to do harm to England',[21] while Gerald of Wales was happy to tell the Pope that: 'Wales is a portion of the kingdom of England, and not a kingdom in itself.'[22] In the mid-thirteenth century, Dafydd ap Llywelyn's appeal to Rome that he should be allowed to hold his lands direct of the Pope and not from Henry III was greeted with outrage by the chronicler Matthew Paris, who asked: 'What Christian can be ignorant that the prince of Wales was a petty vassal of the king of England?'[23]

This mocking tone adopted by English sources would not have been lost on the Welsh leaders who came after Gruffudd ap Llywelyn, nor on their learned subjects. The native clergy had thrived under the great king's patronage and protection, and their references to Gruffudd are almost universally positive. The Welsh chronicle called him 'the foremost of the Britons' and the 'head, shield and defender' of his race. The *Life of St Gwynllyw* described him as 'valiant king of all Wales',[24] while the Book of Llandaff takes an almost imperial tone in its reference to '*rege Grifido monarchia britonum prepollente*' ('King Gruffudd, sole and preeminent ruler of the British').[25] The title 'king of the Britons' had emerged in the native chronicle to describe Wales' greatest leaders and had been applied to Anarawd ap Rhodri, Hywel Dda, Maredudd ab Owain and Llywelyn ap Seisyll before Gruffudd. After 1063, the Welsh chronicle associates just three more men with a claim to this title. The first was Gruffudd's successor

Bleddyn, although it has been seen that the chronicle stressed that his status was inferior to that of his half-brother.[26] The next man to be given the honorific epithet was from a very different heritage: William the Conqueror being described after his death in 1087 as 'prince of the Normans and king of the Saxons and the Britons and the Scots'.[27] In Welsh mythology the title 'king of the Britons' had been held by members of that race since they came to the island from Troy and conquered the giants, and to bestow such a moniker on an outside monarch must have left the learned chronicler with a keen sense of shame. The despair increased in 1093 when Rhys ap Tewdwr was defeated and killed by a Norman army near Aberhonddu (Brecon), the chronicle stating that 'then fell the kingdom of the Britons'. Rhys is the last man that the chronicle associates with the position of 'king of the Britons', although he is not explicitly given that title. In the twelfth century, Geoffrey of Monmouth would claim that the title 'king of the Britons' was given up after the death of Cadwaladr the Blessed in 682, with the original inhabitants of the land then taking on the name 'Welsh'.

The surviving Welsh dynasties would slowly regroup in the course of the twelfth century, notably in Gwynedd under the descendants of Gruffudd ap Cynan. Men like Gruffudd's son, Owain Gwynedd, and his thirteenth-century descendants, Llywelyn ab Iorwerth and Llywelyn ap Gruffudd, would revive the ambition seen so clearly under Gruffudd ap Llywelyn, to rule all of Wales. By their day, however, most of the richest lowlands in the south-east and south-west of the country had been irretrievably lost to Anglo-Norman, French and Flemish invaders from England, while eastern border conquests on the scale that Gruffudd had made in the eleventh century were never a realistic possibility when faced with the ever-growing power of the Anglo-Norman state. In these straitened circumstances, and with outside observers ridiculing the status of Welsh kings, ambitious native nobles adopted the novel title of prince (W. *tywysog*, L. *princeps*) in order to set them apart from their fellow 'kings'. When Owain Gwynedd consciously adopted this style in the 1160s, Beverley Smith has stressed that he was at the height of his power and was still calling himself King of Gwynedd. Owain added the moniker 'prince' in order to reflect his position as leader of the wider Welsh nation.[28] While this may reflect growing Welsh confidence in the later twelfth century, it is impossible not to see the decline in the country's status and aspirations when compared to the time of Gruffudd. The constitutional position sought by Owain Gwynedd was developed by his grandson Llywelyn ab Iorwerth at the start of the thirteenth century, the latter seeing all the native lords of Wales as his tenants. Llywelyn, his son Dafydd and his grandson Llywelyn ap Gruffudd would seek to have this position recognised and ratified by a treaty with the King of England. Inherent in their plan was the direct feudal lordship of the King of England over the Prince of Wales, leaving it clear that the 'kingship of the Britons' was to be sought in London, not in the west of the country. The fact that the thirteenth-century principality of Gwynedd was a part of the kingdom of England and its leader one of the king's magnates was acknowledged by all;[29] no one would have passed such a judgement on Gruffudd ap Llywelyn in his lifetime, nor on the kingdom of Wales that he had forged.

Epilogue

The conquest of 1066 meant disaster for the proud noble lines that had dominated southern Britain since the fall of Rome. Those dynasties, both Welsh and Anglo-Saxon, were soon living under the Norman yoke. In 1093 the last pretender to Gruffudd ap Llywelyn's position as King of the Britons, Rhys ap Tewdwr, was killed in battle by the Norman Bernard de Neufmarché, who was the husband of Gruffudd's granddaughter. The death of Rhys, the son of Gruffudd's old rival Hywel ab Edwin's cousin, opened the way for the Normans to cut a swath across Wales to the Irish Sea and, in the words of the native chronicle, 'then fell the kingdom of the Britons'.[30] The calamity was described in a Latin poem composed by a Welsh cleric from a distinguished and learned family, writing at Llanbadarn Fawr *c.* 1094–95.[31] Rhigyfarch ap Sulien describes himself as 'born of the famous race of the Britons' and his 'Lament' is a fitting epitaph to the world of Gruffudd, and to that of the men who had treacherously engineered his death:

> Why does the earth not consume us, nor the sea swallow us ...
> One vile Norman intimidates a hundred natives with his command, and
> terrifies (them) with his look ...

Families do not now take delight in offspring; the heir does not hope for paternal estates; the rich man does not aspire to accumulate flocks ...

Our limbs are cut off, we are lacerated, our necks condemned to death, and chains are put on our arms.

The honest man's hand is branded by burning metals. A woman (now) lacks her nose, a man his genitals ...

O (Wales), you are afflicted and dying, you are quivering with fear, you collapse, alas, miserable with your sad armament ...

An alien crowd speaks of you as hateful ...

Patriotism and the hope of self-government flee; liberty and self-will perish.[32]

Notes

1. N. Davies, *The Isles: A History* (Oxford, 2000), pp.223–4.
2. *Age*, p.24.
3. See Barlow, *Godwins*, p.82.
4. Barlow, *Edward*, p.244.
5. Examples from 1065 and 1066 are cited below, but the alliance continued beyond this date. Bleddyn and Rhiwallon (until his death in 1069) sought to maintain their vital Mercian alliance, standing by Edwin and Morcar until they were crushed by William the Conqueror, and supporting the Shropshire nobleman Eadric the Wild in his doomed revolt against Norman rule.
6. It has been suggested that Harold may have even been in on the planning of the coup against Tostig. See I. Walker, *Harold: The Last Anglo-Saxon King* (Stroud, 1997), p.235.
7. *Ibid.*, pp.122–3.
8. See Barlow, *Godwins*, pp.72, 79.
9. Stenton, *Anglo-Saxon*, p.581.
10. Barlow, *Godwins*, p.130.
11. *ASC* (D), 1063.
12. See pp.32, 48, 53, 62–6.
13. Domesday Book, Cheshire, folio 263a.
14. *Policraticus*, p.114.
15. *Journey*, p.88.
16. *Ibid.*
17. See J. Gillingham, 'The context and purposes of Geoffrey of Monmouth's

History of the Kings of Britain', *ANS*, 13 (1990), 99–118; *idem* 'The beginnings of English imperialism', *Journal of Historical Sociology*, 5 (1992), 392–409; W.R. Jones, 'England against the Celtic fringe: A study in cultural stereotypes', *Journal of World History*, 13 (1971), 155–71; *idem*, 'The image of the barbarian in medieval Europe', *Comparative Studies in Society and History*, 13 (1971), 376–407.

18. D. Crouch, *The Image of Aristocracy in Britain, 1000–1300* (London, 1992), p.86.

19. *Journey*, p.94.

20. 'Jordan Fantosme: Chronicle of the war between the English and the Scotch in 1173 and 1174', in R. Howlett (ed. and trans.), *Chronicles of the Reigns of Stephen, Henry II and Richard I*, Vol. III (London, 1886).

21. T. Appleby (ed.), *The Chronicle of Richard of Devizes of the time of King Richard the First* (London, 1963).

22. H.E. Butler (ed. and trans.), *The Autobiography of Giraldus Cambrensis* (London, 1937), p.183.

23. J.A. Giles (ed. and trans.), *Matthew Paris' English History*, 3 vols (London, 1852–54).

24. *Vitae*, p.87.

25. J.G. Evans and J. Rhys (ed.), *Liber Landavensis. The Text of the Book of Llan Dav* (Oxford, 1893), p.266; *LL*, pp.535–6.

26. *Brut* (RBH), s.a. 1116. Orderic Vitalis acknowledged Gruffudd's successor as the 'great king Bleddyn', although this was in the context of lauding a victory that was won over the Welshman by Robert of Rhuddlan – see OV, IV, VIII, p.145.

27. *Brut* (RBH), s.a. 1087.

28. Smith, *Llywelyn*, pp.15–18, 283. In Deheubarth, the power of leaders like Rhys ap Gruffudd saw experimentation with the title 'Lord' (W. *arglwydd*); see R. Turvey, *The Lord Rhys, Prince of Deheubarth* (Llandysul, 1997).

29. Smith, *Llywelyn*, p.278.

30. *Brut* (RBH), s.a. 1093. John of Worcester echoes this description with the words 'from that day kings ceased to rule in Wales'.

31. The poet's father's name was Sulien (1011–91). He was Bishop of St David's towards the end of his life and his home and library are thought to have been at the monastery of Llanbadarn Fawr. He was a known patron of Welsh culture and a man who is likely to have played a significant role in the glorification of both Gruffudd and his father, Llywelyn, in the Welsh chronicle.

32. M. Lapidge, 'The Welsh-Latin Poetry of Sulien's Family', *Studia Celtica*, 8/9 (1973–74), 68–106/89–93.

BIBLIOGRAPHY

Printed Sources

Adam of Bremen, *History of the Archbishops of Hamburg-Bremen*, ed. and trans. F.J. Tschan (New York, 1959)

A Mediaeval Prince of Wales: The Life of Gruffudd ap Cynan, ed. and trans. D. Simon Evans (Llanerch, 1990)

Anglo-Saxon Chronicle, ed. and trans. D. Whitelock (London, 1961)

Annala Uladh: Annals of Ulster; otherwise Annals Senait, Annals of Senat; A Chronicle of Irish affairs from AD 431 to AD 1540, ed. and trans. W.M. Hennessy and B. MacCarthy, 4 vols (Dublin, 1887–1901)

Annales Cambriae, ed. J. Williams ab Ithel (Rolls Series, London, 1860)

Annales Monastici, ed. H.R. Luard, 5 vols (Rolls Series, London, 1864–69)

Annals of Clonmacnoise, being Annals of Ireland from the earliest period to AD 1408, translated into English by Connell Mageoghagan, ed. D. Murphey (Dublin, 1896)

Annals of Loch Ce: A chronicle of Irish affairs from AD 1014 to AD 1590, ed. and trans. W.M. Hennessy, 2 vols (London, 1871)

Annals of Tigernach, ed. and trans. W. Stokes, *Review Celtique*, 16 (1895–97)

Annals of Ulster (to AD 1131), part 1, ed. S. MacAirt and G. Mac Niocaill (Dublin, 1983)

Armes Prydein o Lyfr Taliesin, ed. I. Williams (Cardiff, 1955), Eng. vers. R. Bromwich (Dublin, 1972)

Beginnings of Welsh Poetry, The, ed. I. Williams and R. Bromwich, 2nd edn (Cardiff, 1980)

Black Book of Carmarthen, ed. and trans. M. Pennar (Llanerch, 1989)

Bosco, N., 'Dafydd Benfras and his *Red Book* poems', *Studia Celtica*, 22 (1987), 49–117

Brenhinedd y Saeson or The Kings of the Saxons, ed. and trans. T. Jones (Cardiff, 1971)

Breuddwyd Maxen, ed. I. Williams, 3rd edn (Bangor, 1928)

Breudwyt Ronabwy, ed. G.M. Richards (Cardiff, 1948)

Brut y Tywysogyon, Peniarth Ms. 20 Version, ed. T. Jones (Cardiff, 1941)

Brut y Tywysogyon or The Chronicle of the Princes, Peniarth Ms. 20 Version, ed. and trans. T. Jones (Cardiff, 1952)

Brut y Tywysogyon or the Chronicle of the Princes, Red Book of Hergest Version, ed. and trans. T. Jones (Cardiff, 1955)

Calendar of Ancient Correspondence Concerning Wales, ed. J.G. Edwards (Cardiff, 1935)

Calendar of Ancient Petitions Relating to Wales in the Public Record Office, ed. W. Rees (Cardiff, 1975)

Canu Aneirin, ed. I. Williams (Cardiff, 1938)

Canu Llywarch Hen, ed. I. Williams (Cardiff, 1935)

Canu Taliesin, ed. I. Williams (Cardiff, 1960), Eng. vers. J.E. Caerwyn Williams (Dublin, 1968)

Cartae et alia Munimenta de Glamorgan, ed. and trans. G.T. Clark, 6 vols (Talygan, 1910)

Charters of the Abbey of Ystrad Marchell, The, ed. G.C.G. Thomas (Aberystwyth, 1997)

Chronicle of Pierre de Langtoft, ed. T. Wright, 2 vols (London, 1866–68)

Chronicles of the Reigns of Stephen, Henry II, and Richard I, ed. R. Howlett, 4 vols (Rolls Series, London, 1884–89)

Chronicum Scottorum. A chronicle of Irish affairs from the earliest times to AD 1135; with a supplement containing the events from 1141 to 1150, ed. and trans. W.M. Hennessy (London, 1866)

Clancy, J.P., *The Earliest Welsh Poetry* (London, 1970)

Cronica de Wallia, in T. Jones (ed.), 'Cronica de Wallia and other documents from the Exeter Cathedral Library Ms. 3514', *BBCS*, 12 (1946–48), 27–44

Culhwch ac Olwen, ed. R. Bromwich and D. Simon Evans (Cardiff, 1992)

Cyfranc Lludd a Llevelys, ed. I. Williams, 2nd edn (Bangor, 1932)

Cyfreithiau Hywel Dda o Lawysgrif Coleg y Iesu Rhydychen LVII, ed. M. Richards (Cardiff, 1990)

Cyfres Beirdd y Tywysogion, ed. R.G. Gruffydd, 7 vols (Cardiff, 1991–96)

Damweiniau Colau, ed. D. Jenkins (Aberystwyth, 1973)

Davies, S., *The Mabinogion* (Oxford, 2007)

Domesday Book 15, Gloucestershire, ed. J.S. Moore (Chichester, 1982)

Domesday Book 17, Herefordshire, ed. F. and C. Thorn (Chichester, 1983)

Domesday Book 26, Cheshire, ed. P. Morgan (Chichester, 1978)

Earldom of Gloucester Charters. The Charters and Scribes of the Earls and Countesses of Gloucester to AD 1217, ed. R.B. Patterson (Oxford, 1973)

English Historical Documents II, ed. and trans. D.C. Douglas and G.W. Greenway, 2nd edn (London, 1981)

Facsimile of the Chirk Codex of the Welsh Laws, ed. J. Gwenogvryn Evans (Llanbedrog, 1908)

Flores Historiarum, ed. H.R. Luard, 3 vols (Rolls Series, London, 1890)

—, ed. and trans. C.D. Yonge, 2 vols (London, 1853)

Geoffrey of Monmouth, *The History of the Kings of Britain*, ed. and trans. L. Thorpe (Harmondsworth, 1968)

Gerald of Wales, *Journey through Wales, Description of Wales*, ed. and trans. L. Thorpe (Harmondsworth, 1978)

Henry of Huntingdon, *Historia Anglorum*, ed. and trans. D. Greenway (Oxford, 1996)

'Historia Brittonum' and the 'Vatican' Recension, The, ed. D.M. Dumville (Cambridge, 1985)

Historia Gruffud vab Kenan, ed. D. Simon Evans (Cardiff, 1977)

John of Salisbury, *Historia Pontificalis*, ed. M. Chibnall (Edinburgh, 1956)

—, *The Letters of John of Salisbury, Volume One: The Early Letters (1153–61)*, ed. and trans. W.J. Millor and H.E. Butler (Edinburgh, 1955)

—, *The Letters of John of Salisbury, Volume Two: The Later Letters (1163–80)*, ed. and trans. W.J. Millor and C.N.L. Brooke (Oxford, 1979)

—, *Policraticus*, ed. C.J. Nederman (Cambridge, 1990)

John of Worcester, *The Chronicle of John of Worcester*, ed. R.R. Darlington and P. McGurk, trans. J. Bray and P. McGurk, 3 vols (Oxford, 1995)

Jones, G., *The Oxford Book of Welsh Verse in English* (Oxford, 1983)

Jones, T., 'The Black Book of Carmarthen *Stanzas of the Grave*', PBA, 53 (1967), 97–137

Latin Redaction 'A' of the Law of Hywel, ed. and trans. I.F. Fletcher (Aberystwyth, 1986)

Latin Texts of the Welsh Laws, ed. H.D. Emanuel (Cardiff, 1967)

Law of Hywel Dda, ed. and trans. D. Jenkins (Llandysul, 1986)

Laws of Hywel Dda, ed. and trans. M. Richards (Liverpool, 1954)

Liber Landavensis, ed. J.G. Evans (Oxford, 1893)

—, ed. and trans. W.J. Rees (Llandovery, 1840)

Life of King Edward (who rests at Westminster, attributed to a monk of Saint Bertin), ed. and trans. F. Barlow, 2nd edn (Oxford, 1992)

Llandaff Episcopal Acta, 1140–1287, ed. D. Crouch (Cardiff, 1988)

Lloyd, J.E., 'The text of manuscripts 'B' and 'C' of *Annales Cambriae* for the period 1035–93 in parallel columns', THSC (1899–1900), 165–79

Llyfr Blegywryd, ed. S.J. Williams and J.E. Powell, 3rd edn (Cardiff, 1961)

Llyfr Colan, ed. D. Jenkins (Cardiff, 1963)

Llyfr Iorwerth, ed. A.R. Williams (Cardiff, 1960)

Mabinogion, The, ed. and trans. J. Gantz (Harmondsworth, 1976)

New Translated Selections from the Welsh Medieval Law Books, ed. and trans. D. Jenkins (Aberystwyth, 1973)

Orderic Vitalis, *Historia Ecclesiastica*, ed. and trans. M. Chibnall, 6 vols (Oxford, 1969–80)

'Owein' or 'Chwedyl Iarlles y Ffynnawn', ed. R.L. Thomson (Dublin, 1968)

Owen, A., *Ancient Laws and Institutions of Wales*, 2 vols (London, 1841)

Pedeir Keinc y Mabinogi, ed. I Williams (Cardiff, 1930)

Penguin Book of Welsh Verse, The, ed. and trans. A. Conran (Harmondsworth, 1967)

Poetry of Llywarch Hen, The, ed. and trans. P.K. Ford (London, 1974)

Rhigyfarch, *Life of St David*, ed. and trans. J.W. James (Cardiff, 1967)

Richter, M., 'A new edition of the so-called *Vita Davidis Secundi*', *BBCS*,
    22 (1967), 245–9

Roger of Howden, *Annals of Roger de Hoveden*, ed. and trans. H.T. Riley, 2 vols
    (London, 1853)

—, *Magistri Rogeri de Houedene*, ed. W. Stubbs, 4 vols (Rolls Series, London,
    1868–71)

Roger of Wendover, *Flores Historiarum*, ed. H.G. Hewlett, 3 vols (Rolls Series,
    London, 1886–89)

—, *Flowers of History*, ed. and trans. J.A. Giles, 2 vols (London, 1849)

Rowland, J., *Early Welsh Saga Poetry* (Cambridge, 1990)

Salmon, M., *A Source Book of Welsh History* (Oxford, 1927)

Taliesin, *The Poems of Taliesin*, ed. and trans. M. Pennar (Tern Press, 1989)

The Itinerary of John Leland in or about the years 1535–1543, vol. II, ed. L. Toulmin
    Smith (London, 1964),

Thomson, D.S., *Branwen Uerch Lyr* (Dublin, 1961)

Thomson, R.L., *Pwyll Pendeuic Dyvet* (Dublin, 1957)

Trioedd Ynys Prydein / The Welsh Triads, ed. and trans. R. Bromwich, 2nd edn
    (Cardiff, 1978)

Vita Ædwardi Regis, ed. and trans. F. Barlow (1962)

Vitae Sanctorum Britanniae et Genealogiae, ed. and trans. A.W. Wade-Evans (Cardiff,
    1944)

Wade-Evans, A.W. (ed. and trans.), 'Hystoria o Uuched Beuno', *Arch. Camb.*,
    85 (1930), 315–41

Walter Map, *De Nugis Curialium / Courtiers' Trifles*, ed. and trans. M.R. James,
    C.N.L. Brooke and R.A.B. Mynors (Oxford, 1983)

Welsh Life of St David, The, ed. D. Simon Evans (Cardiff, 1988)

Welsh Poems, Sixth Century to 1600, ed. and trans. G. Williams (London, 1973)

Welsh Verse, ed. and trans. T. Conran (2nd edn, Southampton, 1986)

William of Malmesbury, *Gesta Regum Anglorum / The History of the English Kings*,
    ed. and trans. R.A.B. Mynors, R.M. Thomson and M. Winterbottom (Oxford,
    1998)

—, *Historia Novella*, ed. and trans. K.R. Potter (Edinburgh, 1955)

Williams, D.H., *Welsh History through Seals* (Cardiff, 1982)

Secondary Works

Abels, R.P., *Lordship and Military Obligation in Anglo-Saxon England* (London,
    1988)

—, and B.S. Bachrach (eds), *The Normans and their Adversaries at War: Essays in
    Memory of C. Warren Hollister* (Woodbridge, 2001)

Alcock, L., *Dinas Powys* (Cardiff, 1963)

—, *Economy, Society and Warfare among the Britons and Saxons* (Cardiff, 1987)

—, 'Excavations at Castell Bryn Amlwg', *Montgomeryshire Collections*, 60 (1967–68), 8–27

—, 'Excavations at Degannwy Castle, Caernarfonshire, 1961–6', *Archaeological Journal*, 124 (1967), 190–201

Arnold, C.J., Huggett, J.W., and Pryce, H., 'Excavations at Mathrafal, Powys, 1989', *The Montgomeryshire Collections*, 83 (1995), 59–74

—, and J.W. Huggett, 'Pre-Norman rectangular earthworks in mid-Wales', *Medieval Archaeology*, 39 (1995), 171–4

Austin, D., *Carew Castle Archaeological Report*, 1992 Season Interim Report (Lampeter, 1993)

Avent, R., *Castles of the Princes of Gwynedd* (Cardiff, 1983)

—, 'Castles of the Welsh princes', *Château Gaillard*, 16 (1992), 11–20

Babcock, R.S., 'Imbeciles and Normans: The *ynfydion* of Gruffudd ap Rhys reconsidered', *Haskins Soc. Journal*, 4 (1992), 1–10

—, 'Rhys ap Tewdwr, King of Deheubarth', *ANS*, 16 (1993), 21–35

Bachrach, B.S., 'Some observations on the military administration of the Norman Conquest', *ANS*, 8 (1985), 1–26

—, 'The feigned retreat at Hastings', *Mediaeval Studies*, 33 (1971), 264–7

—, 'The practical use of Vegetius' *De Re Militari* during the Middle Ages', *The Historian*, 27 (1985), 239–55

—, *Warfare and Military Organization in Pre-crusade Europe* (Aldershot, 2002)

Barlow, F., *Edward the Confessor* (London, 1989)

—, *The Godwins* (Harlow, 2002)

Barrow, G.W.S., 'Wales and Scotland in the Middle Ages', *WHR*, 10 (1980–81), 302–19

Bartlett, R., *Gerald of Wales, 1146–1223* (Oxford, 1982)

—, and A. Mackay (eds), *Medieval Frontier Societies* (Oxford, 1989)

—, 'Technique militaire et pouvoir politique, 900–1300', *Annales: Economies-Sociétés-Civilisations*, 41 (1986), 1135–59

—, *The Making of Europe* (London, 1993)

Bassett, S. (ed.), *The Origins of Anglo-Saxon Kingdoms* (Leicester, 1989)

Bates, D., 'Normandy and England after 1066', *EHR*, 104 (1989), 851–76

—, *Normandy before 1066* (Harlow, 1982)

—, *William the Conqueror* (London, 1989)

Baxter, S., 'The death of Burgheard son of Ælfgar and its context', in P. Fouracre and D. Ganz (eds), *Frankland. The Franks and the World of the Early Middle Ages. Essays in honour of Dame Jinty Nelson* (Manchester, 2008), pp.266–84

—, *The Earls of Mercia: Lordship and Power in Late Anglo-Saxon England* (Oxford, 2007)

Beeler, J., *Warfare in England, 1066–1189* (New York, 1966)

—, *Warfare in Feudal Europe, 730–1200* (New York, 1971)

Bennett, M., '*La Regle du Temple* as a military manual, or how to deliver a cavalry charge', in Harper-Bill, *Studies*, pp.7–20

141

—, 'The medieval warhorse reconsidered', *Medieval Knighthood*, V (1994), 19-40

Beresford, G., 'Goltho Manor, Lincolnshire: The building and surrounding defences, c.850-1150', *ANS*, 4 (1981), 13-36

Binchy, D.A., *Celtic and Anglo-Saxon Kingship* (Oxford, 1970)

Bloch, M., *Feudal Society*, 2nd edn (London, 1965)

Blockley, K., 'Excavations at Forden Gaer', *Montgomeryshire Collections*, 78 (1990)

Bradbury, J., 'Battles in England and Normandy, 1066-1154', in *ANW*, pp.182-93

—, *The Medieval Archer* (Woodbridge, 1985)

Breeze, A., 'The *Anglo-Saxon Chronicle* for 1053 and the killing of Rhys ap Rhydderch', *Transactions of the Radnorshire Society*, 71 (2001), 168-9

Bromberg, E.I., 'Wales and the mediaeval slave trade', *Speculum*, 17 (1942), 263-9

Bromwich, R., and Brinley Jones, R., *Astudiaethau ar yr Hengerdd* (Cardiff, 1978)

—, *Medieval Welsh Literature to c.1400 including Arthurian Studies* (Cardiff, 1996)

—, Jarman, A.O.H., and Roberts, B.F. (eds), *The Arthur of the Welsh* (Cardiff, 1991)

Brooke, C.N.L., *The Church and the Welsh Border in the Central Middle Ages* (Woodbridge, 1986)

Burgess, E.M., 'The mail-maker's techniques and further research into the construction of mail garments', *Antiquaries Journal*, 33 (1953), 48-55, 193-202

Campbell, E., 'Carew Castle', *Archaeology Wales* 30 (1990)

—, *et al.*, 'Excavations at Longbury Bank, Dyfed, and early medieval settlement in south Wales', *Medieval Archaeology*, 37 (1993), 15-77

—, and Lane, A., 'Llangorse: A tenth-century royal crannog in Wales', *Antiquity*, 63 (1989), 675-81

—, Lane, A., and Redknap, M., 'Llangorse crannog', *Archaeology in Wales*, 30 (1990), 62-3

Charles, B.G., *Old Norse Relations with Wales* (Cardiff, 1934)

Charles-Edwards, T.M., *Early Irish and Welsh Kinship* (Oxford, 1993)

—, Owen, M.E., and Russell, P. (eds), *The Welsh King and his Court* (Cardiff, 2000)

—, *The Welsh Laws* (Cardiff, 1989)

Contamine, P., *War in the Middle Ages* (London, 1984)

Coplestone-Crow, 'Robert de la Haye and the lordship of Gwynllwg: The Norman settlement of a Welsh *cantref*', *Gwent Local History*, 85 (1998), 3-46

Cowley, F., *Gerald of Wales and Margam Abbey*, Friends of Margam Abbey Annual Lecture (1982)

—, *The Monastic Order in South Wales, 1066-1349* (Cardiff, 1977)

Crane, P., 'Iron Age promontory fort to medieval castle? Excavations at Great Castle Head, Dale, Pembrokeshire, 1999', *Arch. Camb.*, 148 (1999), 86-145

Crouch, D., 'The earliest original charter of a Welsh king', *BBCS*, 36 (1989), 125-31

—, *The Image of Aristocracy in Britain, 1000-1300* (London, 1992)

—, 'The slow death of kingship in Glamorgan', *Morgannwg*, 29 (1985), 20-41

Curry, A., 'Review article: Medieval warfare, England and her continental neighbours, eleventh-fourteenth centuries', *Journal of Medieval History*, 24 (1998), 81-102

Dark, K.R., *Civitas to Kingdom: British Political Continuity, 300–800* (Leicester, 1994)

Davidson, H.R.E., *The Sword in Anglo-Saxon England* (Oxford, 1962)

Davies, J.R., 'Church, property and conflict in Wales, AD 600–1100', *WHR*, 18 (1997), 387–406

Davies, N., *The Isles: A History* (Oxford, 2000)

Davies, R.R., *Domination and Conquest* (Cambridge, 1990)

—, *The Age of Conquest: Wales 1063–1415* (Oxford, 1991)

— (ed.), *The British Isles 1100–1500: Comparisons, Contrasts and Connections* (Edinburgh, 1988)

—, 'The peoples of Britain and Ireland, 1100–1400', *TRHS*, 4–7 (1994–97)

Davies, Sean, 'Anglo-Welsh warfare and the works of Gerald of Wales' (unpublished MA thesis, University of Wales Swansea, 1996)

—, 'Native Welsh Military Institutions, c.633-1283' (unpublished PhD thesis, Cardiff, 2000)

—, 'The Battle of Chester and warfare in post-Roman Britain', *History*, 95 (2010), 143–58

—, 'The teulu c.633–1283', *WHR*, 21 (2003), 413–54

—, *Welsh Military Institutions, 633–1283* (Cardiff, 2004)

Davies, Sioned, *The Four Branches of the Mabinogi* (Llandysul, 1993)

—, and N.A. Jones (eds), *The Horse in Celtic Culture: Medieval Welsh Perspectives* (Cardiff, 1997)

Davies, T.M., 'Aspects of medieval landscape change in Herefordshire, Shropshire and Gloucestershire: Evidence from the feet of fines' (unpublished PhD thesis, Newport, 2000)

—, 'Gruffudd ap Llywelyn: An eleventh-century king' (unpublished MA thesis, Cardiff, 1994)

—, 'Gruffudd ap Llywelyn, King of Wales,' *WHR*, 21 (2002), 207–48

—, 'The coming of the Normans', in M. Aldhouse-Green and R. Howell (eds), *The Gwent County History Vol. 1, Gwent in Prehistory and Early History* (Cardiff, 2004)

Davies, W., 'Braint Teilo', *BBCS*, 26 (1974–76), 123–37

—, 'The consecration of the bishops of Llandaff in the tenth and eleventh centuries', *BBCS*, 26 (1974–76), 64–6

—, 'Land and power in early medieval Wales', *P&P*, 81 (1978), 3–23

—, '*Liber Landavensis*: Its construction and credibility', *EHR*, 88 (1973), 335–51

—, *Patterns of Power in Early Wales* (Oxford, 1990)

—, and Fouracre, P. (eds), *Property and Power in the Early Middle Ages* (Cambridge, 1995)

—, *The Llandaff Charters* (Aberystwyth, 1979)

—, *Wales in the Early Middle Ages* (Leicester, 1982)

Davis, P., *Castles of Dyfed* (Llandysul, 1987)

—, *Castles of the Welsh Princes* (Swansea, 1988)

Davis, R.H.C., *The Medieval Warhorse* (London, 1989)

—, *The Normans and their Myth* (London, 1976)

Delbrück, H., *History of the Art of War*, trans. W.J. Renfroe, 4 vols (London, 1982)

DeVries, K., *The Norwegian Invasion of England in 1066* (Woodbridge, 2003)

Diverres, A., 'Can the episode of Arthur's hunt of Twrch Trwyth be an early twelfth century allegory?', *THSC* (1992)

Douglas, D.C., *William the Conqueror* (London, 1964)

Duby, G., *Chivalrous Society* (London, 1977)

Duffy, S., 'Ostmen, Irish and Welsh in the eleventh century', *Peritia*, 9 (1995), 378–96

Dumville, D.M., *Celtic Britain in the Early Middle Ages* (Woodbridge, 1980)

—, *Histories and Pseudo-Histories of the Insular Middle Ages* (Aldershot, 1990)

—, 'Nennius and the *Historia Brittonum*', *Studia Celtica*, 10–11 (1975–76), 78–95

—, 'review of K. Hughes, *The Welsh Latin Chronicles*,' *Studia Celtica*, 12–13 (1977–78), 461–67

—, 'Sub-Roman Britain: History and legend', *History*, 62 (1977), 173–92

Edwards, N., and Lane, A. (eds), *Early Medieval Settlements in Wales, AD 400–1100* (Cardiff, 1988)

— (ed.), *Landscape and Settlement in Medieval Wales* (Oxford, 1997)

—, and Lane, A. (eds), *The Early Church in Wales and the West* (Oxford, 1992)

Ellis, T.P., *Welsh Tribal Law and Custom in the Middle Ages*, 2 vols (Oxford, 1926)

Evans, S.S., *The Lords of Battle: Image and Reality in the 'Comitatus' in Dark-Age Britain* (Woodbridge, 1997)

Fanning, S., 'Tacitus, *Beowulf* and the *comitatus*', *The Haskins Society Journal*, 9 (1997), 17–38

Finberg, H.P.R. (ed.), *The Agrarian History of England and Wales*, I (Cambridge, 1972)

Foster, I.L., and David, G. (eds), *Prehistoric and Early Wales* (London, 1965)

Fox, C., *Offa's Dyke* (Oxford, 1955)

France, J., *Western Warfare in the Age of the Crusades, 1000–1300* (London, 1999)

Garnett, G., and Hudson, J. (eds), *Law and Government in Medieval England and Normandy: Essays in Honour of Sir James Holt* (Cambridge, 1994)

Gillingham, J., 'Conquering the barbarians: War and chivalry in twelfth-century Britain', *Haskins Soc. Journal*, 4 (1992), 67–84

—, *Richard Coeur de Lion: Kingship, Chivalry and War in the Twelfth Century* (London, 1994)

—, 'The beginnings of English imperialism', *Journal of Historical Sociology*, 5 (1992), 392–409

—, 'The context and purposes of Geoffrey of Monmouth's *History of the Kings of Britain*', *ANS*, 13 (1990), 99–118

—, 'The travels of Roger of Howden and his views of the Irish, Scots and Welsh', *ANS*, 20 (1997), 151–69

—, and Holt, J.C. (eds), *War and Government in the Middle Ages: Essays in Honour of J. O. Prestwich* (Woodbridge, 1984)

Given, J., *State and Society in Medieval Europe: Gwynedd and Languedoc Under Outside Rule* (New York, 1990)

Golding, B., 'Gerald of Wales and the monks', *Thirteenth-Century England*, 5 (1993), 53–64

Grabowski, K., and Dumville, D.M., *Chronicles and Annals of Medieval Ireland and Wales* (Woodbridge, 1984)

Gregson, N., 'The multiple estate model: Some critical questions', *Journal of Historical Geography*, 11 (1985), 339–51

Gresham, C.A., 'Aberconway charter', *BBCS*, 30 (1982–83), 311–47

Griffiths, M., 'Native society on the Anglo-Norman frontier: The evidence of the Margam charters', *WHR*, 14 (1988–89), 179–216

Griffiths, R.A. (ed.), *Boroughs of Medieval Wales* (Cardiff, 1978)

—, *Conquerors and Conquered in Medieval Wales* (Stroud, 1994)

Gruffydd, G., and Owen, H.P., 'The earliest mention of St David?', *BBCS*, 17 (1956–58), 185–93

—, and Owen, H.P., 'The earliest mention of St David?: An addendum', *BBCS*, 19 (1960–62), 231–2

Harper-Bill, C. (ed.), *Studies in History Presented to R. Allen-Brown* (Woodbridge, 1989)

Hawkes, S.C. (ed.), *Weapons and Warfare in Anglo-Saxon England* (Oxford, 1989)

Higham, N.J., *An English Empire* (Manchester, 1995)

—, 'Medieval overkingship in Wales: The earliest evidence', *WHR*, 16 (1992–93), 145–59

Higham, R., and Barker, P., *Timber Castles* (London, 1992)

Hill, D., 'The construction of Offa's Dyke', *Antiquaries Journal*, 65 (1985), 140–2

Hogg, A.H.A., and King, D.J. Cathcart, 'Early castles in Wales and the Marches', *Arch. Camb.*, 112 (1963), 77–124

Holden, B.W., 'The making of the middle march of Wales, 1066–1250', *WHR*, 20 (2000), 207–26

Hollister, C.W., *Anglo-Saxon Military Institutions* (Oxford, 1962)

—, *The Military Organisation of Norman England* (Oxford, 1965)

Holm, P., 'The slave trade of Dublin, ninth–twelfth centuries', *Peritia*, 5 (1986), 317–45

Hooper, N., 'Anglo-Saxon warfare on the eve of the Norman Conquest', *ANS*, 1 (1978), 84–93

—, 'The Aberlemno stone and cavalry in Anglo-Saxon England', *Northern History*, 29 (1993), 188–96

—, and Bennett, M. (eds), *The Cambridge Illustrated Atlas of Warfare: The Middle Ages, 768–1487* (Cambridge, 1996)

Hopkinson, C., 'The Mortimers of Wigmore, 1086–1214', *TWNFC*, 46 (1989), 177–93

— 'The Mortimers of Wigmore, 1214–82', *TWNFC*, 47 (1993), 28–46

Hudson, B.T., 'The destruction of Gruffudd ap Llywelyn', *WHR*, 15 (1990–91), 331–50

Hughes, K., 'The Welsh-Latin chronicles: *Annales Cambriae* and related texts', *PBA*, 57 (1973), 233–58

Hyland, A., *The Medieval Warhorse from Byzantium to the Crusades* (Stroud, 1994)

Insley, C., 'Kings, lords, charters and the political culture of twelfth-century Wales', ANS, 30 (2007), 133–54

Jackson, K.H., *Language and History in Early Britain* (Edinburgh, 1953)

James, J.W., 'Fresh light on the death of Gruffudd ap Llywelyn', BBCS (1982), 147

Jankulak, K. and Wooding, J.M. (eds), *Ireland and Wales in the Middle Ages* (Dublin, 2007)

Jarman, A.O.H., and Hughes, G.R. (eds), *A Guide to Welsh Literature* (Cardiff, 1992)

Jarrett, M.G., *Early Roman Campaigns in Wales*, Seventh Annual Caerleon Lecture (Cardiff, 1994)

Johnstone, N., '*Llys* and *Maerdref*: The royal courts of the princes of Gwynedd', *Studia Celtica*, 34 (2000), 167–210

Jones, E.D., 'The locality of the battle of Mynydd Carn, AD 1081', *Arch. Camb.*, 77 (1922), 181–97

—, Davies, N.G. and Roberts, R.F., 'Five Strata Marcella charters', *NLWJ*, 5 (1947–48), 50–4

Jones, G.R.J., 'Multiple estates perceived', *Journal of Historical Geography*, 11 (1985), 352–63

—, 'The defences of Gwynedd in the thirteenth century', *TCHS*, 30 (1969), 29–43

—, 'The distribution of bond settlements in north-west Wales', *WHR*, 2 (1964–65), 19–36

—, 'The military geography of Gwynedd in the thirteenth century' (unpublished MA thesis, University of Wales Aberystwyth, 1949)

—, 'The models for organisation in *Llyfr Iorwerth* and *Llyfr Cyfnerth*', *BBCS*, 39 (1992), 95–118

—, 'The pattern of settlement on the Welsh border', *Agricultural History Review*, 8 (1960), 66–81

—, 'The tribal system in Wales', *WHR*, 1 (1960–63), 111–32

Jones, N.A., and Pryce, H. (eds), *Yr Arglwydd Rhys* (Cardiff, 1996)

Jones, R., 'The formation of the *cantref* and the commote in medieval Gwynedd', *Studia Celtica*, 32 (1998), 169–77

Jones, W.R., 'England against the Celtic fringe: A study in cultural stereotypes', *Journal of World History*, 13 (1971), 155–71

—, 'The image of the barbarian in medieval Europe', *Comparative Studies in Society and History*, 13 (1971), 376–407

Jones, W.R.D., 'The Welsh rulers of Senghennydd', *Caerphilly*, 3 (1971), 9–19

Jones-Pierce, T., *Medieval Welsh Society*, ed. Smith, J.B. (Cardiff, 1972)

Kenyon, J.R., and Avent, R. (eds), *Castles in Wales and the Marches* (Cardiff, 1987)

—, 'Fluctuating frontiers: Normano-Welsh castle warfare, c.1075–1240', *Château Gaillard*, 17 (1996), 119–26

King, D.J. Cathcart, 'The defence of Wales, 1067–1283: The other side of the hill', *Arch. Camb.*, 126 (1977), 1–16

Kirby, D.P., 'Hywel Dda: Anglophile?', *WHR*, 8 (1976–77), 1–13

Knight, J.K., 'Welsh fortifications of the first millennium AD', *Château Gaillard*, 16 (1992), 277–84

Koch, H.W., *Medieval Warfare* (London, 1978)

Lapidge, M., 'The Welsh-Latin poetry of Sulien's family', *Studia Celtica*, 8–9 (1973–74), 68–106

Lawson, M.K., *Cnut* (London, 1993)

Lewis, C.P., 'English and Norman government and lordship in the Welsh borders, 1039–87' (unpublished D.Phil. thesis, Oxford University, 1985)

—, 'The French in England before the Norman Conquest', *ANS*, 17 (1994), 123–44

—, 'The Norman settlement of Herefordshire under William I', *ANS*, 7 (1984), 195–213

Lewis, C.W., 'The treaty of Woodstock, 1247: Its background and significance', *WHR*, 2 (1964–65), 37–65

Lewis, S., *A Topographical Dictionary of Wales*, II, 4th edn (London, 1849)

Lloyd, J.E., *A History of Wales from the Earliest Times to the Edwardian Conquest*, 2 vols, 3rd edn (London, 1939)

—, 'The Welsh chronicles', *PBA*, 14 (1928), 369–91

—, 'Wales and the coming of the Normans', *THSC* (1899–1900), 122–79

Lloyd-Jones, J., 'The court poets of the Welsh princes', *PBA*, 34 (1948), 167–97

Longley, D., 'The excavations of Castell, Porth Trefadog: A coastal promontory fort in north Wales', *Medieval Archaeology*, 35 (1991), 64–85

Loyd, L.C., *The Origins of Some Anglo-Norman Families* (Leeds, 1951)

Loyn, H.R., *The Vikings in Wales* (London, 1976)

—, 'Wales and England in the tenth century: The context of the Athelstan charters', *WHR*, 10 (1980–81), 283–301

Ludlow, N., 'The castle and lordship of Narberth', *The Journal of the Pembrokeshire Historical Society*, 12 (2003), 5–43

Mac Cana, P., *Celtic Mythology* (London, 1970)

—, *The Mabinogi* (Cardiff, 1992)

Manley, J., 'The late Saxon settlement of Cledemutha (Rhuddlan), Clwyd', in Faull, M.L. (ed.), *Studies in Late Anglo-Saxon Settlement* (Oxford, 1984)

—, 'Rhuddlan', *Current Archaeology*, 7 (1982), 304–7

Mann, K.J., 'King John, Wales and the March' (unpublished Ph.D. thesis, University of Wales Swansea, 1991)

Marshall, G., 'The Norman occupation of the lands in the Golden Valley, Ewyas and Clifford and their motte and bailey castles', *TWNFC* (1936–38), 141–58

Mason, E., 'Change and continuity in eleventh-century Mercia: The experience of St Wulfstan of Worcester', *ANS* 8 (1985)

Maund, K.L., 'Cynan ab Iago and the killing of Gruffudd ap Llywelyn', *CMCS*, 10 (1985), 57–65

—, 'Dynastic segmentation and Gwynedd c.950–c.1000', *Studia Celtica*, 32 (1998), 155–67

— (ed.), *Gruffudd ap Cynan: A Collaborative Biography* (Woodbridge, 1996)

—, *Handlist of the Acts of Native Welsh Rulers, 1132–1283* (Cardiff, 1996)

—, *Ireland, Wales and England in the Eleventh Century* (Woodbridge, 1991)

—, 'The Welsh alliances of Earl Ælfgar of Mercia and his family in the mid-eleventh century', *ANS*, 11 (1988), 181–90

—, *The Welsh Kings: The Medieval Rulers of Wales* (Stroud, 2000)

—, 'Trahaearn ap Caradog: Legitimate usurper?', *WHR*, 13 (1986–87), 468–76

Mayr-Harting, H., and Moore, R.I. (eds.), *Studies in Medieval History Presented to R.H.C. Davis* (London, 1985)

McCann, W.J., 'The Welsh view of the Normans', *THSC* (1991), 39–67

McGlynn, S., 'The myths of medieval warfare', *History Today*, 44 (1994), 28–34

McNeill, T., *Castles in Ireland: Feudal Power in a Gaelic World* (London, 1997)

Miles, H., 'Rhuddlan', *Current Archaeology*, 3 (1972), 245–8

Miller, M., 'Bede's use of Gildas', *EHR*, 90 (1975), 245–61

Morillo, S., 'review of Suppe, *Military Institutions*,' *Trans. Shropshire Arch. and Hist. Soc.*, 70 (1995), 218–19

—, *Warfare Under the Anglo-Norman Kings, 1066–1135* (Woodbridge, 1994)

Morris, J.E., *The Welsh Wars of Edward I* (Oxford, 1901, new edn Stroud, 1996)

Musson, C.R., and Spurgeon, C.J., 'Cwrt Llechryd, Llanelwedd: An unusual moated site in central Powys', *Medieval Archaeology*, 32 (1988), 97–109

Nash-Williams, V.E., *The Roman Frontier in Wales* (Cardiff, 1954)

Nelson, L.H., *The Normans in South Wales, 1070–1171* (Austin, Texas, 1966)

Nicolle, D., *Medieval Warfare Source Book: Vol. 1, Warfare in Western Christendom* (London, 1995)

Oakeshott, R.E., *The Sword in the Age of Chivalry* (London, 1964)

Ó'Cróinín, D., *Early Medieval Ireland, 400–1200* (Harlow, 1995)

Oman, C., *A History of the Art of War in the Middle Ages, 378–1485* (Oxford, 1991)

Owen, D.H. (ed.), *Settlement and Society in Wales* (Cardiff, 1989)

Parker, G., *The Cambridge Illustrated History of Warfare* (Cambridge, 1995)

Petts, D., *The Early Medieval Church in Wales* (Stroud, 2009)

Pierce, G.O., 'The evidence of place-names', in *Glamorgan County History*, III, pp.456–92

Pierce, I., 'Arms, armour and warfare in the eleventh century', *ANS*, 10 (1987), 237–58

—, 'The knight, his arms and armour in the eleventh century', *Medieval Knighthood*, I (1986), 157–64

Powel, D., *The Historie of Cambria* (London, 1584, facsimile edn, Amsterdam, 1969)

Power, R., 'Magnus Barelegs' expeditions to the west', *Scottish Historical Review*, 65 (1986), 107–32

Powicke, M.R., *Military Obligations in Medieval England* (Oxford, 1962)

Preston-Jones, A., and Rose, P., 'Medieval Cornwall', *Cornish Archaeology*, 25 (1986), 135–85

Pryce, H., 'Ecclesiastical wealth in early medieval Wales', in Edwards and Lane, *Early Church*, pp.22–32

—, 'In search of a medieval society: Deheubarth in the writings of Gerald of Wales', *WHR*, 13 (1986–87), 265–81

—, 'Owain Gwynedd and Louis VII: The Franco-Welsh diplomacy of the first Prince of Wales', *WHR*, 19 (1998), 1–28

—, 'The church of Trefeglwys and the end of the 'Celtic' charter tradition in twelfth-century Wales', *CMCS*, 25 (1993), 15–54

Radford, C.A.R. and Hemp, W.J., 'The cross-slabs at Llanrhaiadr-ym-Mochnant', *Arch. Camb.* 106 (1957), 109–16

Rahtz, P., 'Hereford', *Current Archaeology*, 9 (1968), 242–6

Rees, S.E., and Caple, C., *Dinefwr Castle and Dryslwyn Castle* (Cardiff, 1996)

Rees, W., *A Historical Atlas of Wales from Early to Modern Times* (Cardiff, 1951)

Remfry, P.M., 'Cadwallon ap Madog, Rex de Delvain, 1140–79, and the re-establishment of local autonomy in Cynllibiwg', *Trans. Radnorshire Soc.*, 65 (1995), 11–32

—, 'The native Welsh dynasties of Rhwng Gwy a Hafren, 1066–1282' (unpublished M.Phil. thesis, University of Wales Aberystwyth, 1989)

Roderick, A.J., 'Feudal relations between the English Crown and the Welsh princes', *History*, 37 (1952), 201–12

Rowland, J., 'Old Welsh *franc*: An Old English borrowing?', *CMCS*, 26 (1993), 21–5

—, 'Warfare and horses in the *Gododdin* and the problem of Catraeth', *CMCS*, 30 (1995), 13–40

Rowlands, I.W., 'The 1201 peace between King John and Llywelyn ap Iorwerth', *Studia Celtica*, 34 (2000), 149–66

—, 'The making of the March. Aspects of the Norman settlement in Dyfed', *ANS*, 3 (1980), 142–58

—, 'William de Braose and the lordship of Brecon', *BBCS*, 30 (1982–83), 123–33

Ryan, J., 'A study of horses in early and medieval Welsh literature, *c*.600–1300 AD' (unpublished M.Phil. thesis, University of Wales Cardiff, 1993)

Savory, H.N., 'Excavations at Dinas Emrys, Beddgelert, 1954–6', *Arch. Camb.*, 109 (1960), 13–78

Sawyer, P.H., *The Age of the Vikings* (2nd edn, London, 1971)

—, and Hayes, P. (eds), *The Oxford Illustrated History of the Vikings* (Oxford, 1997)

Schenfeld, E.J., 'Anglo-Saxon *burhs* and continental *burgen*: Early medieval fortifications in continental perspective', *Haskins Soc. Journal*, 6 (1994), 49–66

Schubert, H.R., *History of the British Iron and Steel Industry* (London, 1957)

Scragg, D.C. (ed.), *The Battle of Maldon, AD 991* (Oxford, 1991)

Seebohm, F., *The Tribal System in Wales*, 2nd edn (London, 1904)

Shoesmith, R., 'Hereford', *Current Archaeology*, 24 (1971), 256–8

Simms, K., *From Kings to Warlords* (Woodbridge, 1987)

Sims-Williams, P., 'Historical need and literary narrative: A caveat from ninth-century Wales', *WHR*, 17 (1994–95), 1–40

Smail, R.C., *Crusading Warfare* (Cambridge, 1956)

Smith, J.B., 'Land endowments of the period of Llewelyn ap Gruffudd', *BBCS*,
  34 (1987), 150–64

—, 'Llywelyn ap Gruffudd and the March of Wales', *Brycheiniog*, 20 (1982–83), 9–22

—, *Llywelyn ap Gruffudd, Prince of Wales* (Cardiff, 1998)

—, 'Llywelyn ap Gruffudd, Prince of Wales and Lord of Snowdon', *TCHS*,
  45 (1984), 7–36

—, 'Magna Carta and the charters of the Welsh princes', *EHR*, 99 (1984), 344–62

—, 'Owain Gwynedd', *TCHS*, 32 (1971), 8–17

—, 'The kingdom of Morgannwg and the Norman conquest of Glamorgan', in
  Glamorgan County History, III, pp.1–44

—, 'The lordship of Glamorgan', *Morgannwg*, 9 (1965), 9–38

—, and Pugh, T.B., 'The lordship of Gower', in *Glamorgan County History*, III,
  pp.205–83

—, 'The middle March in the thirteenth century', *BBCS*, 24 (1970), 77–93

Smith, L.B., 'The *gravamina* of the community of Gwynedd against Llywelyn ap
  Gruffudd', *BBCS*, 31 (1984), 158–76

Squatriti, P., 'Digging ditches in early medieval Europe,' *P&P*, 176 (2002), 11–65

Stenton, F., *Anglo-Saxon England* (Oxford, 2001)

Stephenson, D., *The Governance of Gwynedd* (Cardiff, 1984)

—, 'Powis Castle: A reappraisal of its medieval development, *Montgomeryshire
  Collections*, 95 (2007), 9–22

—, 'The politics of Powys Wenwynwyn in the thirteenth century', *CMCS*,
  7 (1984), 39–61

—, 'The resurgence of Powys in the late eleventh and early twelfth centuries',
  ANS, 30 (2007), 182–96

—, 'The whole land between Dyfi and Dulas', *Montgomeryshire Collections*,
  95 (2007), 1–8

Strange, W.A., 'The rise and fall of a saint's community: Llandeilo Fawr,
  600-1200', *Journal of Welsh Religious History*, 2 (2002), 1–18

Strickland, M. (ed.), *Anglo-Norman Warfare* (Woodbridge, 1992)

—, 'Military technology and conquest: The anomaly of Anglo-Saxon England',
  ANS, 19 (1996), 353–82

—, *War and Chivalry: The Conduct and Perception of War in England and Normandy,
  1066–1217* (Cambridge, 1996)

Suppe, F.C., 'Interpreter families and Anglo-Welsh relations in the
  Shropshire-Powys marches in the twelfth century', *ANS*, 30 (2007), 196–212

—, *Military Institutions on the Welsh Marches: Shropshire, AD 1066–1300* (Woodbridge,
  1994)

—, 'The cultural significance of decapitation in high medieval Wales and the
  Marches', *BBCS*, 36 (1989), 147–60

—, 'Roger of Powys, Henry II's Anglo-Welsh middleman, and his lineage',
  WHR, 21 (2002), 1–23

—, 'Who was Rhys Sais? Some comments on Anglo-Welsh relations before
  1066', *Haskins Soc. Journal*, 7 (1995), 63–73

Thordemann, B., *Armour from the Battle of Wisby, 1361*, 2 vols (Stockholm, 1939)

Thornton, D.E., 'Maredudd ab Owain (d.999): The most famous king of the Welsh', *WHR*, 18 (1997), 567–91

—, 'Who was Rhain the Irishman?', *Studia Celtica*, 34 (2000), 131–48

Turvey, R., 'Llandovery Castle and the Pipe Rolls (1159–62)', *The Carmarthenshire Antiquary*, 26 (1990), 5–12

—, *Llywelyn the Great* (Llandysul, 2007)

—, 'The death and burial of an excommunicate prince: The Lord Rhys and the Cathedral Church of St Davids', *Journal Pembs. Hist. Soc.*, 7 (1996–97), 26–49

—, 'The defences of twelfth-century Deheubarth and the castle strategy of the Lord Rhys', *Arch. Camb.*, 144 (1995), 103–32

—, *The Lord Rhys, Prince of Deheubarth* (Llandysul, 1997)

Van Houts, A.E., 'The Norman Conquest through European eyes', *EHR*, 110 (1995), 832–53

Verbruggen, J.F., *The Art of Warfare in Western Europe in the Middle Ages* (New York, 1977)

Wainwright, F.T., 'Cledemutha', *EHR*, 65 (1950), 203–12

Walker, D., 'A note on Gruffudd ap Llywelyn', *WHR*, 1 (1960–63), 83–94

—, 'William fitz Osbern and the Norman settlement in Herefordshire', *TWNFC*, 39 (1967–69), 402–12

Walker, I.W., *Harold, the Last Anglo-Saxon King* (Stroud, 1997)

—, *Mercia and the Origins of England* (Stroud, 2000)

Warrington, W., *The History of Wales* (4th edn, Brecon, 1823)

White, S.D., 'Kinship and lordship in early medieval England: The story of Sigeberht, Cynewulf and Cyneheard', *Viator*, 20 (1989), 1–18

Whitelock, D., *et al.* (eds), *The Norman Conquest* (London, 1966)

Wilkinson, P.F., 'Excavations at Hen Gastell, Briton Ferry, West Glamorgan, 1991–2', *Medieval Archaeology*, 39 (1995), 1–50

Williams, A.G., 'Norman lordship in south-east Wales during the reign of William I', *WHR*, 16 (1992–93), 445–66

—, 'The Norman lordship of Glamorgan: An examination of its establishment and development' (unpublished M.Phil. thesis, University of Wales Cardiff, 1991)

Williams, A.R., 'Methods of manufacture of swords in medieval Europe', *Gladius*, 13 (1977), 75–101

—, 'The knight and the blast furnace', *Metals and Materials*, 2 (1986), 485–9

—, 'The manufacture of mail in medieval Europe: A technical note', *Gladius*, 15 (1980), 105–34

Williams, J.E. Caerwyn, *The Poets of the Welsh Princes* (Cardiff, 1994)

Williams-Jones, K., 'Llywelyn's charter to Cymer Abbey in 1209', *Journal Merioneth Hist. Soc.*, 3 (1957), 45–78

Woolf, R., 'The ideal of men dying with their lords in the *Germania* and the Battle of Maldon', *Anglo-Saxon England*, 5 (1976), 69–81

Wyatt, D., 'Gruffudd ap Cynan and the Hiberno-Norse world,' *WHR*, 19 (1999), 595–617

INDEX